Scotland's Approach to Regulating Water Charges

INNOVATION AND COLLABORATION

This document, as well as any data and map included herein, are without prejudice to the status of or sovereignty over any territory, to the delimitation of international frontiers and boundaries and to the name of any territory, city or area.

Please cite this publication as:
OECD (2022), *Scotland's Approach to Regulating Water Charges: Innovation and Collaboration*, The Governance of Regulators, OECD Publishing, Paris, https://doi.org/10.1787/fcc8c6df-en.

ISBN 978-92-64-78579-3 (print)
ISBN 978-92-64-89111-1 (pdf)
ISBN 978-92-64-59493-7 (HTML)
ISBN 978-92-64-54093-4 (epub)

The Governance of Regulators
ISSN 2415-1432 (print)
ISSN 2415-1440 (online)

Foreword

The price regulation conducted by economic regulators is a high-stakes process, with significant and lasting effects: prices are often set for a multi-year period and have wide, tangible impacts. Price regulation influences investment in infrastructure maintenance and upgrades, and can facilitate the transition to a low-carbon economy and society. Ultimately, price regulation affects the daily lives of citizens, impacting household bills and influencing the quality of services households receive. At its best, price regulation has the potential to position the regulated sector to contribute to long-term goals and policies, and remain resilient to future shocks.

This report, the result of a multi-year peer review, discusses the efforts of the economic regulator of the Scottish water sector (the Water Industry Commission of Scotland, WICS) to make the results of its price-setting process work better for the customers of today and tomorrow. The price-setting process (the Strategic Review of Charges for 2021-2027, or SRC21) launched in 2017. Involving close collaboration between WICS and sector stakeholders, it confronted issues relating to sustainable asset management, intergenerational equity and climate change. Understanding customer views became even more important in tackling these major and inherent regulatory challenges; better capturing and relaying customer views into decision making became a focus of the process.

The review finds that parties consider the price-setting process a success. It built stakeholder buy-in on major strategic issues, such as managing assets and meeting a net-zero greenhouse gas emissions objective in the sector. In addition, a new focus on collaboration, openness and trust has strengthened the overall regulatory system. The system has shown its resilience, shifting direction when faced with new challenges such as the COVID-19 crisis and the introduction of a net-zero goal for Scottish Water.

WICS and other stakeholders faced uncertainty head-on as they completed a different type of price review, and they are again contending with some uncertainty as they implement a modified regulatory framework. Defining milestones, demonstrating progress, and maintaining opportunity for constructive challenge will lay foundations for greater stability and predictability in the regulatory framework. In addition, parties should not lose sight of strategic vision and goals, which can provide a guiding beacon as parties navigate uncharted waters.

While certain aspects of the price review are unique to Scotland, many of the themes underlying SRC21 touch upon questions core to modern economic regulation:

- Regulatory frameworks focus on the regulatory period, sometimes at the expense of long-term needs, including for infrastructure. **How can economic regulators better incorporate consideration of long-term goals for sustainable asset management within the regulatory cycle?**
- As countries continue to increase their ambition to tackle the climate challenge, changes in approach will affect all parts of the public service. **How will economic regulators and the network sectors they regulate contribute to public efforts for climate adaptation and mitigation?**

- Many public bodies struggle to engage with a broad swathe of customers and communities; at the same time, many citizens report low levels of trust in public institutions. **Can regulators engage better with customers and communities to improve decision making and trust?**

In taking the first steps towards answering these questions, the price-setting process in the Scottish water sector gives valuable information about what it means to be an economic regulator, and what it looks like to regulate better in the face of contemporary challenges.

This report is part of the OECD work programme on the governance of regulators and regulatory policy, led by the OECD Network of Economic Regulators and the OECD Regulatory Policy Committee, with the support of the Regulatory Policy Division of the OECD Public Governance Directorate. The Directorate's mission is to help government at all levels design and implement strategic, evidence-based and innovative policies that support sustainable economic and social development. The report was presented to the OECD Network of Economic Regulators for comments and approval at its 17th meeting in November 2021 and declassified by written procedure by the Regulatory Policy Committee on 4 January 2022. It was prepared for publication by the Secretariat.

Acknowledgements

This report was prepared by the OECD Public Governance Directorate (GOV) under the leadership of Elsa Pilichowski, Director. It was co-ordinated by Alexis Durand and drafted by Alexis Durand and Filippo Cavassini, with inputs from Nick Malyshev and Anna Pietikäinen. Special thanks go to Lorenzo Casullo and Faisal Naru for their significant contributions to earlier versions of the draft and their work leading up to this version. The report was prepared with the encouragement and support of János Bertók, Deputy Director, GOV, and Nick Malyshev, Head of the Regulatory Policy Division, GOV. Jennifer Stein co-ordinated the editorial process and Andrea Uhrhammer provided editorial support.

The team benefited from the expertise of peer reviewers, who participated in four in-person and virtual missions to Scotland and provided extensive inputs and feedback throughout the development of the review: Adam Wilson, Chief Executive Officer, the Essential Services Commission of South Australia; Ulrike Britton, Chief Director, Development and Infrastructure, National Treasury of South Africa; Jean-Yves Ollier, *Maître des requêtes*, the French Supreme Court for administrative law (*Conseil d'État*); and Anne Yvrande Billon, Director of Economy, Markets and Digital at the French regulatory authority for electronic communications, postal services and press distribution (*L'Autorité de régulation des communications électroniques, des postes et de la distribution de la presse, Arcep*), who participated as a peer from 2017-2020.

The report would not have been possible without the support of WICS, its staff, and other participants in the SRC21 process since the beginning of the engagement in 2017. The team would like to thank in particular the following colleagues at WICS for their valuable assistance in collecting data and information, for their support and flexibility in organising and conducting the team's missions remotely, as well as for providing feedback at different stages of the review: Alan Sutherland (Chief Executive), Donald MacRae (Chair of the Commission), Jo Armstrong (Board Member), Ian Tait (Deputy Chief Executive), David Satti (Assistant Director), Colin McNaughton (Assistant Director), Donna Very (Assistant Director), Claire Nichols (Assistant Director), Stephanie Capaldi (Communications and Central Office Manager), Joanne Burns (Senior Business Support Officer), and Marie Gardner (Senior Business Support Officer).

SRC21 benefited from the enthusiasm and dedication of participants and observers to the process, and the same can be said for this review. The authors would like to thank the following individuals for participating in interviews and providing comments, and for their openness throughout the review. From the Scottish Government: Jon Rathjen (Deputy Director, Water Policy & Climate Change and Energy Directorate Operations) and Bob Irvine (former Deputy Director Climate Change & Water Industry). From Scottish Water: Douglas Millican (Chief Executive Officer), Simon Parsons (Director of Strategic Customer Service Planning), Tom Harvie-Clark (General Manager of Strategy and Economic Regulation), Brian Lironi (Director of Corporate Affairs), Molly Horsley (Senior Lead, Customer), and Rob Mustard (Director of Digital). From the Scottish Environment Protection Agency: Jennifer Leonard (Water Industry Planning Unit Manager) and Nathan Critchlow-Watton (State of Environment Unit Manager). From the Customer Forum: Sam Ghibaldan (Director), Peter Peacock (former Chair), and Agnes Robson (former Chair). From Citizens Advice Scotland: Gail Walker (Water Policy Team Manager). From the Drinking Water Quality Regulator for Scotland: Sue Petch (Drinking Water Quality Regulator). The OECD team also met with other institutions and individuals over the years and would like to thank all for their time and inputs to the review.

Table of contents

FIGURES

TABLES

Follow OECD Publications on:

Abbreviations and acronyms

CAA	UK Civil Aviation Authority
CAS	Citizens Advice Scotland
CFU	Consumer Futures Unit
CLCV	Consommation, logement et cadre de vie
CPI	Consumer price index
CRE	Commission de régulation de l'énergie
DAG	Delivery Assurance Group
DWQR	Drinking Water Quality Regulator
EBP	Ethical business practice
EBR	Ethical business regulation
EBRSG	EBR Support Group
ERSE	Energy Services Regulatory Authority of Portugal
ESCOSA	Essential Services Commission of South Australia
European Union	EU
ICG	Independent Customer Group
IPPF	Investment Planning and Prioritisation Framework
IPPG	Investment Planning and Prioritisation Group
OMG	Output Monitoring Group
RCG	Research Co-ordination Group
RPI	Retail price index
SAG	Stakeholder advisory group
SEPA	Scottish Environmental Protection Authority
SRC	Strategic Review of Charges
SRC15	Strategic Review of Charges 2015-2020
SRC21	Strategic Review of Charges 2021-2027
UNIDEN	L'Union des Industries Utilisatrices d'Énergie
WG	Working group
WICS	Water Industry Commission for Scotland

Executive summary

The Water Industry Commission for Scotland (WICS) is the economic regulator of the Scottish water sector. Economic regulation has brought significant benefits to the sector, including improved efficiency and customer focus by the publicly owned Scottish Water, the single operator in the household market, and effective retail competition in the non-household market.

Through processes called "Strategic Reviews of Charges" (or SRCs), WICS sets water charges over a six-year regulatory period, within parameters set by government policies. In the Strategic Review of Charges 2021-2027 (SRC21) process, WICS saw the opportunity to fundamentally re-think the regulatory approach to tackle interrelated challenges: regulating better for customers of today and tomorrow; addressing challenges associated with long-life assets and a lack of flexibility for investment; addressing a perceived adversarial approach in regulation; and maximising opportunities for the consumer voice to feed into decision making.

The result of SRC21 has been a substantial shift in the regulatory approach for the Scottish water sector, designed to support a more strategic approach to economic regulation and a better production and use of data and analysis to inform investment decisions. The revamped regulatory framework allows greater flexibility in investment choices and includes incentives for decision making with long-term objectives in mind. Scottish Water, WICS and other actors are developing tools to model Ethical Business Regulation (EBR) and Practice (EBP) in the sector. Scottish Water has redoubled its efforts to increase consumer and community engagement in decision making, including through an independent customer group embedded within Scottish Water. Both Scottish Water and WICS have committed to organisational transformation to ensure that they are up to the task.

This shift has introduced a degree of uncertainty, notably with the move from periodically fixed capital expenditure and deliverables towards rolling investment decisions, and requires systemic culture change for successful implementation. As the framework firms up and parties adapt to new roles and ways of working, they should leave space for failure and learning. During this transitional period, parties can lay foundations to improve the stability and predictability of the regulatory framework, such as parameters, roles and milestones, while demonstrating progress towards shared objectives and organisational transformation. At the same time, maintaining opportunities for scrutiny and challenge and capturing the full breadth of views will help ensure that decision making is robust. Throughout this transitional period, parties should keep strategic goals in sight.

Reflections on the SRC21 process

SRC21 evolved to address emerging challenges and was successful in developing a shared vision and strategy for the sector. It adapted to changes in the substantive focus of the price review, such as the 2019 introduction of the net-zero challenge by the Scottish Government. It also adapted to changes in process and outputs, such as a shift to a "strategic plan" as a major output for Scottish Water and the changes in the Customer Forum role.

Parties agreed that SRC21 was "worth it". While continued engagement required high levels of commitment, it produced considerable benefits. SRC21 also resulted in strategic outcomes: a shared commitment around objectives addressing sustainable asset management and climate change, and an emphasis on openness and transparency. Parties are eager to continue maximising the utility of these strategic outcomes during the regulatory period.

The challenges of the present: The delivery period

As SRC21 concludes, parties share clear desired outcomes but are still developing a well-defined route map to attain them. The new approach introduces additional uncertainty, especially for drinking water quality and environmental regulators used to agreeing to fixed capital expenditure and deliverables for investment. A key challenge will be maintaining the confidence of parties and the public and managing expectations.

Scottish Water and WICS have both launched institutional transformation processes. Scottish Water needs to transform a delivery institution into a company embracing principles of openness, customer-centricity, and EBP while achieving long-term objectives including a net-zero target. WICS has acknowledged that a commitment to EBR "takes two", launching its own process of transformation planning. It will be important for this transformation to permeate throughout each organisation and even transcend these institutions to have systemic impact.

Key recommendations

- Defining milestones and checkpoints upfront will help ensure that processes are on track to achieve long-term objectives.
- Clarifying roles will be important in an evolved regulatory framework that is transforming not only the regulated company but also the role of WICS and the other regulators involved in investment planning.
- Visible transformation planning of Scottish Water will need to be accompanied by visible transformation of some of the regulators and skills updating within Scottish Water, its contractors and WICS.
- Engagement with other parties and the public should expand to systematically capture the full breadth of views, allowing diverse voices to be important sources of new data and approaches.

The outlook for the future: The next SRC

Parties invested in "re-inventing" SRC21, but expect the regulatory cycle to become more continuous and seamless going forward. There is now an opportunity to take stock of what is already in place and what is needed before SRC27. Participants should invest in codifying and documenting these roles and providing a roadmap for how to work together, building on the process, groups and mechanisms already in place, which can serve as an input to the SRC27 methodology. These measures will also help the framework remain resistant to changes in participants.

While parties took significant steps to distance themselves from a perceived adversarial approach to regulation, it will be important for a challenge function to remain strong in future SRCs. The delivery period should include ample opportunity for candid and open exchange, including with stakeholders outside of the core group, and to embrace necessary tensions.

Key recommendations

- Early discussion can already set a "no surprises" tone for SRC27 and help parties identify areas where process efficiencies can be realised.
- Parties can build upon the experience of SRC21 to establish firmer expectations earlier in the SRC process.
- Parties should consider how to harness stakeholder, customer, and community input and action for highest impact.

Timeline

Since its launch in early 2017, SRC21 has progressed in the context of an evolving policy environment. The points below highlight key developments in and alongside the SRC process.

Events related to the OECD peer review are highlighted in grey

January 2017	Ministers issue their **Commissioning Letter** to WICS, specifying the deadline for the Final Determination of Charges and outlining Ministers' expectations for the SRC21 arrangements.
March 2017	WICS, Scottish Water and CAS sign a **co-operation agreement** creating the Customer Forum for SRC21. The agreement also provides for a research programme and operational arrangements to coordinate research activities; the Research Coordination Group is created pursuant to these provisions.
April 2017	WICS releases the **methodology** for SRC21, outlining their approach to the SRC21 process. WICS shared refinements to the methodology in autumn 2018 following feedback from stakeholders.
September 2017	The **OECD peer review team** visits Scotland to map the start of the SRC21.
October 2017	Water industry stakeholders hold the first stakeholder meeting to facilitate joint working for the SRC21, leading to the creation of the **Stakeholder Advisory Group**.
February 2018	Scottish Water releases its **Strategic Projections**, defining overarching ambitions to address future challenges and outlining planned actions to help deliver on these ambitions.
April 2018	The **Capital Maintenance Advisory Group,** convened to better understand the actual needs for an appropriate capital programme for SRC21 and further into the future, concludes its first phase of work.
July 2018	Consultation on draft **Principles of Charging and Ministerial Objectives** opens, running until September 2018.
September 2018	**WICS exchanges letters** with Scottish Water and the Customer Forum, laying out further information about the approach to SRC21 and the Strategic Plan.
October 2018	The **OECD peer review team** visits Scotland to map progress of SRC21.
December 2018	Scottish Water releases their **Outline Strategic Plan**, further defining fifteen strategic outcomes within its four overarching ambitions, captured in the 'Strategic Wheel'.
February 2019	The **Ethical Business Regulation (EBR) Support Group** conducts its first assessment.

March 2019	Participants to the Stakeholder Advisory Group co-create a draft **vision for the water industry**: "Scotland's water sector will be admired for excellence, secure a sustainable future and inspire a Hydro Nation."
May 2019	**Working groups** continue their activities and finalise some of their decisions. **Research efforts** continue with the conclusion of behaviourally-informed studies on trade-offs and launch of the deliberative research study aimed at understanding perceptions.
June 2019	The **Cabinet Secretary's keynote address** recognises that a flourishing Scotland needs a flourishing water sector and officially invites stakeholders to propose a vision for the sector.
July 2019	The Scottish Government issues an updated **Commissioning Letter** with indicative price profiles, a stronger emphasis on climate change, and a requirement to create a vision for the sector. Detailed **prioritisation workshops** take place focusing on the 'no regrets' investment components that will make the development lists.
August 2019	WICS publishes their final **Decision Paper on Asset Replacement**, highlighting the likely required levels of investment in light of ageing assets and climate change challenges.
September 2019	The Scottish Government releases its **Programme for Scotland 2019-2020**, which commits Scottish Water to becoming a net-zero carbon user of electricity by 2040, ahead of the overall net-zero emissions commitment for Scotland as a whole in 2045. The **Investment Planning and Prioritisation Group** (IPPG) agrees on its Terms of Reference and meets for the first time. The Group is chaired by the Scottish Government and stakeholders agree that they will work together to endorse the process of investment selection.
November 2019	Following inputs from stakeholders at the Stakeholder Advisory Group and bilateral meetings, Scottish Water presents a **Strategic Plan** to its Board of Directors for approval. The **OECD peer review team** visits Scotland to map progress of SRC21.
January 2020	The government publishes the **draft Ministerial Objectives and Principles of Charging for the water sector** that incorporates the sector vision.
February 2020	Scottish Water publishes their **Strategic Plan**, Our Future Together. The Customer Forum and Scottish Water sign a **Minute of Agreement on the Strategic Plan**, agreeing that the plan reflects customer and community priorities and aspirations and outlining aspects for further development. WICS publishes its final decision paper **Prospects for Prices** with its conclusion that annual average charges must increase by between 1 and 2% above Consumer Price Inflation. The Customer Forum and Scottish Water enter **discussions about prices** for 2021-27.
March 2020	Lockdowns announced in Scotland and the UK as part of the response to the **COVID-19** pandemic. The Customer Forum and Scottish Water reach a **draft agreement on prices** for 2021-27. However, given the uncertainty arising from COVID-19, it was decided to delay decisions on prices until the implications were clearer.
April 2020	At the request of the Scottish Government, WICS seeks input from industry stakeholders on how best to conclude the SRC21 process, given the impacts of the pandemic, and sets out a range of options.

April 2020 | **Chair of the Customer Forum resigns** and is replaced by a new chair.

May 2020 | WICS writes to the Cabinet Secretary regarding the Impact of COVID-19 on the Strategic Review of Charges 2021-27.

September 2020 | The Customer Forum and Scottish Water enter into a minute of agreement on **expectations for the transformation plan and the future of customer involvement**.

October 2020 | The Scottish Government sets out a **revised timetable** for SRC21 in light of the pandemic.

WICS publishes its **draft determination** proposing annual average price increases of CPI+2% over the regulatory period, efficiency challenges, and a ring-fenced allowance to account for externalities in investment decisions, with a six-week comment period.

The **OECD peer review team** is briefed on developments in the SRC21 process.

December 2020 | The Scottish Government published its final **Principles of Charging and Investment** Objectives for the regulatory period, including extensions to the support available through the water charge reduction scheme.

WICS publishes its **final determination**, making slight adjustments to the financial modelling but maintaining the key parameters of the draft determination.

February 2021 | Scottish Water, accepts the final determination and announces its **2021-2022 household charges**. Taking account of the extension to the charges reduction scheme, it includes an average charge increase across all customers of 0.9%, with a 2.5% increase for those paying full charge levels.

May/June 2021 | The OECD Secretariat and peers hold the **final OECD peer mission**.

November 2021 | The OECD peer review is discussed by the **OECD Network Economic Regulators** at its 17th November meeting.

1 Key insights and recommendations

This chapter summarises the key insights and recommendations resulting from the multi-year peer review of Scotland's price-setting process for the water sector (the Strategic Review of Charges for 2021-2027, or SRC21), launched in 2017. It draws lessons from the completed SRC21, identifies lessons for the delivery of SRC21 and looks ahead to next steps on the regulatory journey.

The economic regulator of the Scottish water sector, the Water Industry Commission for Scotland (WICS), is tasked with setting household water charges over the regulatory period within the parameters set by government policies. The Scottish water sector is characterised by the presence of a single state-owned operator in the household market – Scottish Water. By law, WICS engages in a Strategic Review of Charges (SRC) process every six years, and it also has the statutory remit to monitor and report on Scottish Water's performance during the regulatory period. In the liberalised non-household retail market, WICS is tasked with facilitating competition.

While economic regulation had delivered substantial benefits to the Scottish water sector, WICS entered the Strategic Review of Charges 2021-2027 (SRC21) acknowledging some of the limitations of its past approach in the present context. The benefits of economic regulation of the water sector in Scotland have been considerable, including improved efficiency and customer focus by Scottish Water, and effective retail competition since the non-household downstream market was opened to competition in 2008. As it approached SRC21, WICS saw the opportunity to re-think the approach taken in previous SRCs to address a number of interrelated challenges:

- **The limitations of an adversarial approach in regulation:** WICS perceived that, in using the common tools of economic regulation, regulators could inadvertently foster an adversarial relationship between the regulator and the regulated entity. It believed that this relationship could undermine the willingness to share information and be open about the performance of the company and sector. WICS sought to address what was perceived as a key challenge, modifying the regulatory framework to create an open and transparent process for determining investment needs and to minimise dysfunctional behaviour between the actors of the regulatory eco-system. The regulator drew inspiration from ethical business regulation (EBR) and ethical business practice (EBP), explaining that it hoped to no longer rely solely on its regulatory powers of enforcement.

- **Challenges associated with long-life assets and time inconsistency of investment:** Decisions on asset management today can affect consumers decades into the future, making a strategic approach to decision making about long-life assets critical. The existing regulatory framework with a strong focus on six-year price-setting was considered too rigid to allow for consideration of trade-offs between today's costs and future benefits. Going into SRC21, WICS made it clear that it saw a long-term view to asset management as a precondition for the maintenance and improvement of service levels.

  As the SRC continued, a focus on long-term decision making and asset replacement evolved to include consideration of climate change as this issue gained greater prominence. Stakeholders already showed enthusiasm about responding to climate change even before the government's net zero announcement, and this enthusiasm was supported by research suggesting that customers cared about long-term issues like those related to climate change. The need for aligning investment decisions with a long-term perspective became even more urgent after the government set a "beyond net-zero" target for Scottish Water in line with ambitious whole-of-government climate objectives established in the government's Programme for Scotland 2019-2020 (Scottish Government, 2019[1]).

- **Lack of flexibility of investment:** Previous SRCs culminated in an agreement on a list of investment requirements between Scottish Water and the 'quality regulators' (Scottish Environment Protection Agency and the Drinking Water Quality Regulator). Among other limitations, this system encouraged the company to make asset decisions on the basis of lowest monetary costs within the six-year price-setting period. The regulator saw an opportunity to create a more flexible arrangement in which decision making would be made on the basis of highest whole-life value instead of lowest short-term cost. This approach would be expected to help better address the need to take into consideration new long-term investment challenges like those created by climate change, net-zero targets and long-term asset replacement in a more comprehensive fashion.

- **The challenge of embedding the customer and community voice**: The previous regulatory process, SRC15, had created the Customer Forum to negotiate prices with Scottish Water. This had created a new opportunity for customers to provide constructive challenge at the heart of the price setting process. Working closely with the statutory water sector customer body (Citizens Advice Scotland), WICS hoped to build on the success of the Customer Forum for SRC15 by considering new ways to maximise opportunities for the consumer voice to feed into Scottish Water's ongoing decision making and develop further research on customers' understanding of the water industry challenges and customers' preferences.

Faced with these challenges, SRC21 employed new methods and produced a new dynamic for the Scottish water sector. SRC21 prioritised multi-stakeholder discussion to collect information and make decisions. The result was an evolved regulatory framework that moves away from a focus on fixed regulatory periods, a fixed set of investment projects, and a hard budget constraint. Instead, it introduces arrangements to provide flexibility and focus on strategic outcomes. SRC21 united a select group of stakeholders[1] around a long-term vision, and stakeholders expect future SRCs to become check-in points on the route towards long-term objectives. Ultimately, the evolved regulatory framework aims to ensure that the economic regulation of the sector provides the resources to accommodate and protect the needs of customers of today and tomorrow.

This review documents and analyses SRC21, drawing from a multi-year observation on the part of the OECD Secretariat and four peer missions since 2017. These Key insights and recommendations draw lessons from the completed SRC21, identify lessons for the delivery of SRC21 and look ahead to next steps on the regulatory journey. Chapter 2 describes the context of the Scottish water sector, and the events leading up to the start of SRC21. It explains the market structure, introduces key institutions, and summarises previous regulatory periods. Chapter 3 captures and analyses the components and major milestones of SRC21. It is structured around the four interrelated challenges introduced above: 1) the limitations of an adversarial approach, 2) challenges associated with long-life assets and time inconsistency, 3) flexibility of investment, and 4) embedding the customer and community voice.

The formulation of these key insights and recommendations comes after SRC21 formally ended with Scottish Water's acceptance of WICS's Final Determination in January 2021. But the "proof of the pudding is the eating": putting the outputs of SRC21 into action will be the true test of its effectiveness and its innovations. The following insights and recommendations do not aim to provide an answer to the challenges of implementation that ultimately will need to be managed by the SRC parties. They point to the importance of continuing to pose the difficult questions that SRC21 started asking on a wide array of topics. These topics include the challenges of taking a long-term view to address new challenges posed by ageing assets, climate change and net-zero emission targets. As these challenges both originate from and affect the behaviour and understanding of customers and communities, SRC21 highlighted also the even greater importance of engaging with customers, communities and the broader public. Scottish Water's greater ownership of its plans fostered by SRC21 will also impact accountability and the work of regulators, transforming how Scottish Water as well as the economic and quality regulators deliver excellence to customers and communities.

Box 1.1. Civil aviation authorities putting EBR into practice

While many aspects of EBR remain largely untested in the economic regulation context, other regulators have applied the principles underlying EBR in different jurisdictions. One notable example is civil aviation.

Recognising the limits of compliance-based regulation in aviation safety regulation, civil aviation authorities have developed a new approach based on "just and open culture". Certain authorities have

---

put into place mechanisms to enable honest conversations with providers not hindered by fear so as to create a culture of open communication and mutual learning and in which consequences are always visibly implemented.

The UK Civil Aviation Authority has exemplified this shift in its approach to safety regulation. It has moved to a forward-looking, performance-based and principles-based approach that encourages market actors to take responsibility for organisational culture. It has moved away from blame-based, punitive approaches, instead placing emphasis on building trust relationships. (Hodges, 2016[2]) notes the positive impact of these trust relationships, stating that "best airlines regard it as a matter of honour to raise potential issues with responsible regulators swiftly – but also to implement solutions without waiting to be told."

Source: (Hodges and Steinholtz, 2018[3]), The International Adoption of Ethical Business Regulation, Policy Brief, The Foundation for Law, Justice and Society, https://www.fljs.org/sites/default/files/migrated/publications/The%20International%20Adoption%20of%20Ethical%20Business%20Regulation.pdf; (Hodges, 2016[2]), Ethical Business Regulation: Growing Empirical Evidence, Policy Brief, the Foundation for Law, Justice and Society, https://www.fljs.org/sites/default/files/migrated/publications/Ethical%20Business%20Regulation.pdf; Information provided by C. Hodges (2021), and the UK Civil Aviation Authority (2022).

Reflections on the SRC21 process

Expectations for the SRC21 process evolved considerably between the first formal governmental inputs into the SRC process (the Ministerial Objectives and Principles of Charging) and the Final Determination of the regulator. At the beginning of SRC21, stakeholders expected changes to the process to build on the evolution of the previous SRCs, but the extent of those changes were not fully clear or charted. After the conclusion of SRC21, it is clear that the process, outputs and immediate outcomes mark a transformative change in the Scottish context. Within policy directions, SRC21 places new emphasis on sustainable asset management and climate change. The modified regulatory framework emerging from SRC21 supports a more strategic, long-term perspective, replacing a more rigid approach to investment decision making anchored firmly within a single regulatory period.

SRC21's focus adapted to external evolutions, showing the capacity of the more collaborative regulatory framework to respond effectively to policy and market developments. For example, the regulatory framework emerging from SRC21 shows an emphasis on addressing climate change in response to the formal establishment of a 2040 net-zero goal for Scottish Water in mid-2019, as well as enthusiasm from other stakeholders to reduce the footprint of the sector and research suggesting that consumers care about long-term issues like climate change.

Participants in SRC21 also adapted to changes in process and terms of reference. Scottish Water moved from the initial proposal to prepare a 'business plan' for the regulatory period to the development of a "strategic plan". This shift away from an input-output focussed business plan, which would detail investment requirements and Scottish Water's view of necessary financing for delivery, towards a plan with fewer specifics but a greater emphasis on outcomes within a strategic vision presented a new challenge to a company with a historical focus on delivery and least-cost engineering. Also, the role of the Customer Forum shifted significantly twice during SRC21, but the group delivered effectively upon its final mandate. While significant changes did result in some setbacks, such as the resignation of the first chair of the SRC21 Customer Forum, the process showed a degree of resilience to change.

Parties showed leadership in key areas that shaped SRC21's process and outputs. The government set an ambitious policy goal for the company of achieving net zero emissions by 2040 which significantly raised the profile of climate change within the SRC. WICS also showed leadership and a willingness to disrupt the regulatory framework and extend what would normally be the exclusive domain of the regulator to accept input and collaboration from other stakeholders. Scottish Water has shown that it is eager to rise to the challenge presented by SRC21, committing to a major transformation journey.

SRC21 mobilised a high level of engagement and resources especially in terms of staff involvement for some of the parties, but parties agree that the investment was "worth it". SRC21 involved an elevated level of ongoing commitment from stakeholders, who participated in thematic working groups and "deep dive" sessions alongside monthly high-level meetings. At times, the continued engagement stretched the resources of some participants. However, with hindsight, some participants noted that this investment enabled an outcome that was accepted and not contested by any parties. As a counterfactual, the more adversarial approach of previous SRCs had the potential to create significant operational costs associated with the high level of data exchange required and if outputs are contested (for example, in terms of legal and economic consulting), as had previously occurred after the regulator's price determination in 2006. The high level of engagement in SRC21 has allowed WICS to rely less on external consultancy resources, reducing consultancy costs by around 20%, and more on internal staff.

Stakeholders largely agree that the new approaches and ways of working are here to stay. There was a new emphasis on learning during SRC21, which stakeholders appreciated. "Deep dive" sessions allowed stakeholders to understand Scottish Water's business challenges. Another valued outcome is an increased focus on engagement and transparency. SRC21 placed new emphasis on communication, collaboration and sharing, which has been institutionalised in regular meetings of stakeholders. An Ethical Business Regulation Support Group performed a regular "temperature check" of openness and trust during the SRC21 process. A Research Co-ordination Group allowed parties to contribute to a shared body of research. While bilateral stakeholder meetings continued to further progress in some specific areas, multi-lateral meetings and joint research became the norm in SRC21. These new ways of working emphasised openness leading up to the publication of the determination. At the conclusion of SRC21, there was a low likelihood of a formal challenge by Scottish Water of WICS's final determination because the parties had worked together in a closely collaborative process with other stakeholders throughout the SRC21 process. There remains a strong appetite for continued engagement going into the implementation period. Stakeholders recognise that "going back to previous approaches is not an option". In terms of outcomes, stakeholders appreciate the new focus on sustainable infrastructure management and climate change in the final products of SRC21.

Parties made progress towards the open sharing of information in SRC21. For example, Scottish Water held a series of "deep dive" sessions to stakeholders to help all parties understand how the company operates. Scottish Water opening its asset registers for examination by WICS is another example of the greater degree of information sharing achieved in the course of SRC21. Maintaining a rich and transparent data flow between WICS, Scottish Water and other parties, on a no-blame basis, is one element of ethical business regulation that should continue going forward.

SRC21 placed new and urgent policy issues of priority to stakeholders at its centre, and the group has attained a high degree of convergence on the importance of these issues. The centricity of sustainable asset management and climate change in particular differentiates SRC21 from previous SRCs. As SRC21 had embraced a more collaborative way of working, buy-in from stakeholders around these issues would be a determinant of the viability of a modified regulatory framework. SRC21 has successfully developed buy-in around both of these issues among participants, using stakeholder discussion and exchange of evidence. The convergence is perhaps best displayed in the sector vision, where the government, regulator, regulated company and stakeholders express a shared vision that the water sector will be capable of advancing towards these objectives.

The SRC21 research programme, an innovative new programme in the Scottish water sector, produced some unique and impactful research, although it started slowly with a broad mandate. A 'Research Co-ordination Group' had broad scope to produce a range of research products, tasked with producing "high quality, behavioural, quantitative and qualitative research within the context of the SRC to establish customers' priorities for service level improvement and expectations in terms of the level of charges." The group produced numerous studies to feed into SRC21, including through collaboratively-designed studies. However, a structured discussion about research priorities did not begin in earnest until late 2018. The timing of later research, such as the deliberative research conducted in late 2018, partially limited these studies' impact on the proceedings, albeit the key findings – for example on the broad acceptability of price increases – influenced the final outcome.

A Customer Forum again offered the promise of a conduit for customer views into the SRC21 process, although its shifting mandate caused discomfort to forum participants. Building on the success of SRC15, SRC21 again constituted a Customer Forum to reflect customer views in SRC21 decision making. Due to changing circumstances, partly linked to the COVID pandemic, the mandate of the Customer Forum shifted significantly at two junctures during SRC21. The Customer Forum found its functions shifting from (1) agreeing a business plan with Scottish Water to (2) agreeing a 25-year Strategic Plan and a price profile to deliver it within WICS's limits for the SRC21 period, to (3) expressing views on Scottish Water's transformation plan and customer centricity goal. Despite discomfort resulting from a shifting mandate, the Forum produced a summary of its involvement in SRC21 that outlined its major achievements in SRC21. These achievements included the role of the forum in crafting the vision and strategic plan, its early championing for climate change as a key strategic issue, and its role in securing Scottish Water's commitment to customer centricity.

Box 1.2. Customer representation in French energy regulation

A range of tools help the French energy regulator (Commission de régulation de l'énergie, or CRE), government and regulated entities take into account customer interests and preferences in decision making.

Associations play an important role in the French regulatory landscape. A specialised association (L'Union des Industries Utilisatrices d'Énergie, or UNIDEN) represents 50 energy-intensive consumers, accounting for 70% of the French industry consumption. UNIDEN is an active and frequent contributor to consultations and regulatory debates. Fifteen designated associations represent household customers before courts and some public authorities. They have three main origins: family associations, unions, and the consumer movement (with three general associations and three specialist associations for housing and transports). In the absence of relevant specialist associations, the representation of household energy consumers falls to two main general associations (UFC-Que Choisir and Consommation, logement et cadre de vie, or CLCV) and on the individual involvement of critical persons within a few family associations. By way of example, UFC-Que Choisir has played an active role in the opening of markets to competition by grouping domestic retail customers to organise tenders for market offers, has challenged several regulatory decisions before the Council of State, and has supported the regulator's defence against an unsuccessful challenge against the electricity distribution tariff.

The regulator and the government's main regulatory decisions are submitted to the superior energy council, a body (created in 1946) which includes representatives from parliament, government, energy companies, unions, and few consumer representatives. The government serves as its secretariat. Its ability to represent all stakeholders has been challenged, although a 2016 revision of the composition of the council increased the presence of professional and industrial consumers.

Domestic and business customers were represented each by one member within the board of CRE between 2007 and 2011. These appointments were suppressed, the representation as stakeholders within the board being viewed as contradicting the principle of independence of decision bodies. Since

---

2015, one member of the board is appointed in consideration of his or her expertise in the area of consumer protection. CRE also has recruited staff with specific expertise in customer relations.

Consumer associations participate in public consultations and are consulted on the main regulatory decisions. They are members of working groups on market rules and standard contracts, created and maintained by CRE. The two largest general associations tend to focus on decisions relating to end-user regulated tariffs and smart metering. The representation of consumer voices on other key regulatory decisions relies on associations with more limited resources. The regulator's challenge is to provide an appropriate level of assistance and interaction on complex regulatory decisions to ensure that these associations' views are expressed and taken into account.

Consumer perceptions are also measured through enquiries on the quality of service of DSOs and on customer satisfaction. The national energy mediator, which receives complaints on energy services, is also a major channel of customer views, whose partnership with the regulator is critical.

Sources: Contributed by peer reviewer Jean-Yves Ollier, with input from the French energy regulator CRE (2021).

The challenges of the present: The delivery period

Creativity and a willingness to disrupt established practice in the Scottish water sector have paid off during SRC21, but the delivery period will benefit from stability and predictability. Parties put significant energy into "reinventing" the SRC process for SRC21, and the outcomes of SRC21 were enabled by parties' willingness and ability to embrace change. As the regulatory cycle becomes more continuous and seamless, with price reviews being 'check points' in that continuous process rather than the sole focus, the disruptive stage should give way to something more stable, providing stability and certainty to deliver on objectives and outcomes.

As SRC21 concludes, parties share clear desired outcomes but are still in the process of developing a well-defined route map to attain them. Parties have united around a long-term vision of the sector, which was given legal status in the government's final Ministerial Objectives and Principles of Charging. While Scottish Water's 25-year Strategic Plan, agreed upon with the Customer Forum, and WICS's final determination sketch the broad outlines of expectations for implementation, significant uncertainties remain in relation to how these outcomes will be achieved. Some of this uncertainty is by design. The modified regulatory framework changes the role of SRCs: instead of an SRC marking the beginning of a new, stand-alone regulatory period, the SRC will function as a checkpoint in a series of ongoing processes. Instead of well-defined intermediate delivery outputs, the framework allows for decision making on a rolling basis. Other uncertainty comes as a function of the newness of the modified approach: parties are fleshing out the delivery modalities as they go. For example, Scottish Water has a fixed 2040 net-zero goal, and an early roadmap towards the goal provides a broad sketch of activities and outputs to help them attain the objective without providing precise details. Inevitably, it will take a few iterations to come up with operational roadmaps that integrate the objectives of the Strategic Plan and the transformations that parties and the process itself are undertaking.

SRC21 is marked by an expectation that Scottish Water will take full ownership of its decision making and strategy, which places a greater onus on the company to understand statutory obligations and the wider expectations of stakeholders, customers and communities. Scottish Water is still held to a set of statutory standards, and it must work closely and proactively with regulators to understand its binding obligations as well as discretionary choices. Stakeholders look to Scottish Water to own the decisions and strategy that will shape Scottish Water's response to meeting binding obligations, responding to customer and community needs, and striking a balance between competing trade-offs.

Rolling investment planning introduces additional uncertainty, especially for quality regulators. The previous system was designed to promote efficiency, minimising short-term cash costs. It involved a fixed amount of capital expenditure and a fixed list of deliverables, agreed upon by quality regulators and WICS. This provided a high degree of certainty around necessary improvements that would be delivered to achieve regulatory standards. The modified regulatory framework, with investment decision making occurring on a rolling basis, reduces this certainty and moves towards an outcome focus. To provide a degree of certainty around delivery, Scottish Water has written "letters of commitment" stating when the company expects to start and complete certain key projects.

Entering an implementation period marked by a high degree of uncertainty, a key challenge will be maintaining the confidence of parties and the public and to manage expectations. Strong outcome accountability (both in terms of service quality and organisation behaviours) through the entire regulatory system will be one way to maintain confidence and serve as a bulwark against negative outcomes. These types of accountability mechanisms can provide confidence to multiple audiences (including the government, regulators and the public) that the regulatory framework is delivering upon its objectives and that there is no 'regulatory capture'. Demonstrable progress towards organisational transformation planning will also be important to build confidence that parties are making necessary organisational changes to meet the challenges ahead. Accountability will be anchored on candour, trust relationships, and sound analysis, but a shared definition of *what* constitutes each of these foundations will be important to manage expectations.

Scottish Water and WICS have both launched processes of institutional transformation, and the ambition and reach of transformation should meet the scale of the challenges ahead. WICS and Scottish Water have committed to a modified framework that represents a radical change from the Scottish water sector *status quo*, and key questions remain about the magnitude and rate of institutional change necessary to deliver the new framework. Scottish Water, faced with the challenge of transforming what has been a delivery institution into a company embracing the principles of the final determination, launched its transformation planning with a stock-take of its company character and is working with experts and a management consultancy as it develops a transformation plan. A shift towards EBR "takes two," and WICS acknowledged that it requires its own transformation as well as that of the regulated company. WICS has taken the first steps in its own transformation planning, reflecting on necessary adjustments through expert workshops and in its corporate plan. The transformation will require senior leadership to enlist the participation of employees at all levels to ensure that change permeates throughout the organisation, a challenge especially relevant in an institution as large as Scottish Water. In addition, the necessary transformation extends beyond these two organisations, and it is important for this transformation to transcend institutions and reach the system level. The pace of change will also be important, as parties try to transition to a new normal as quickly as possible.

Recommendations

Stakeholders should maintain space in regular stakeholder meetings for strategic, blue-sky thinking. After the conclusion of SRC21, the stakeholder group may shift naturally towards considering areas of greater operational and implementation detail. However, maintaining opportunities for higher-level and strategic discussion on the ongoing development of long-term issues can provide perspective during the implementation phase, as well as collecting views from stakeholders on an ongoing basis in case key strategic parameters shift over time.

Parties should clarify understandings and expectations for customer and community involvement. The terms "customer" and "community" used in key outputs of the SRC21 process encompass a vast range of diverse individuals and groups. Similarly, processes to involve customers and communities are varied and multifaceted. Involving customers and communities involves resources and maintaining multiple channels of information and participation can be complex; a deliberate approach that seeks to develop a shared baseline among involved parties can also help guide actions for greatest impact. Parties could consider undertaking a 'deep dive' into the issue of customer and community engagement early in the regulatory period to develop shared understandings and expectations. Parties can then collectively define how the customers and communities will benefit from a process which more deeply involves their views and how such benefits can best be realised in the Scottish context. Parties can embed structures and relationships within the regulatory system early in the process.

Going forward, parties can gain legitimacy by broadening and strengthening inclusion along the spectrum of public participation. "Informing" the public and interested groups is the most basic action on the spectrum of public participation. SRC21 has focused on developing internal transparency, and efforts to develop external transparency remained limited throughout the process to communication and consultation on a few key outputs, like the draft determination. Providing timely, comprehensible, accessible and relevant information to a broader audience at key decision points can foster a "no surprises" environment beyond parties to SRC21. Beyond providing information, parties to the SRC21 process would benefit from taking advantage of a full range of participation tools to broaden engagement. SRC21 brought together an "inner circle" of core participants, with limited opportunities for "outsiders" to participate. This "inner circle" will continue to an extent in the implementation period, for example with regular meetings of stakeholders. To balance the influence of this core group, participants should ensure that engagement occurs extends beyond the group and adequate feedback is provided to consultation contributors. Deliberative research commissioned by Scottish Water suggested that informed members of the public have clear views on the development of the water industry, showing a potentially rich vein of new perspectives from non-insiders.

Systematically capturing the full breadth of views will allow diverse civil society voices to be an important source of new data and approaches. The Independent Customer Group's (ICG's) promise to be a vehicle for customer and community views hinges on whether it can maintain a strong challenge function and connection to customers and communities. This connection will have to be durable and forward-looking: representing the interests of future customers will require a strong sense of future needs and evolving customer preferences (including of young customers) that will need to be embedded into SW. Parties can "build a bigger tent" using a range of tools beyond existing structures to funnel diverse views and expertise into delivery. The public should have a clear path for meaningful engagement, with clear levels of influence to create realistic expectations. Clarity about the respective responsibilities and capabilities of parties helps give interested parties a clear path to provide input without feeling like parties are "passing the buck."

The visible transformation planning of Scottish Water and WICS is key to develop confidence moving forward – both in (1) the capacity for both organisations to deliver upon their roles in the coming period and (2) the strength of the foundations for EBR and EBP. Scottish Water and WICS have committed to processes of organisational transformation to ensure that the two organisations are able to deliver the desired outcomes of the modified regulatory approach. Scottish Water's transformation has been open to scrutiny by stakeholders as it creates a "transformation plan". Raising the visibility of WICS's own transformation planning will demonstrate the organisation's commitment to its own transformation.

The new approaches in this regulatory period may require updating skills within WICS, Scottish Water and Scottish Water's contractors. While one focus of transformation planning is culture, the necessary institutional shift is not limited to culture change. It also includes updating internal capacities. For example, the regulator and the company will both need to develop skills to adapt to a new system of investment prioritisation. Within the scope of Ministerial Objectives, there will be some hard questions that both organisations will have to answer in terms of possible trade-offs between, for instance, climate change commitments and customer excellence. Along with other relevant regulators and bodies, the regulator has to be well equipped to provide guidance, if necessary, and facilitate genuine dialogue between relevant parties to allow these trade-offs to be addressed. Such a capacity update should be approached proactively, through an analysis of needs, tailored training, and recruitment to fill gaps.

Stakeholders can expect a transition period as certain parties embark on processes of transformation, and should create a safe space for failure and learning. Cultural and operational change will not happen overnight, and transforming programmes may also involve experimentation. Parties can expect hiccups during institutional transformation processes, and a safe space will allow for learning while still supporting openness and transparency consistent with EBR-inspired principles. When it comes to the regulator's response to failure from the regulated company, the regulator should have the ability to identify when there is a risk of material harm to customers and respond accordingly.

Defining milestones and checkpoints upfront will help ensure that processes are on track to achieve long-term objectives. As parties navigate the uncertainty of the modified regulatory framework during the implementation phase, regular checkpoints with agreed milestones linked to both (1) service quality and investment and (2) organisational transformation and behaviours can provide a stabilising effect and serve as an early-warning system if results diverge from expectations. For example, WICS may benefit from further defining the process and metrics of success for Scottish Water's transformation in consultation with all parties. Making certain expectations and evaluation criteria explicit can guide progress and help parties use resources efficiently, while allowing flexibility insofar as it supports EBR and EBP.

WICS and other parties should clarify roles in the context of an evolved regulatory framework that is transforming not only the regulated company but also the role of the regulators. The stakeholder group could benefit from additional clarity on the role of the regulator and other parties in the investment decisions and more strategic decisions going forward. The contours of relationships between parties are also worth re-examining. Clarity on roles and relationships will be a necessary input to (1) establish expectations on where certain functions lie (like those related to broader policy issues), (2) assess the degree to which the framework reflects EBR and EBP, and (3) ensure succession planning across organisations and the system.

Dialogue will need to continue throughout implementation, and structured co-ordination mechanisms can reduce transaction costs going forward. How regulators can continue to work together in the evolved regulatory environment becomes even more important during the coming period. Continued dialogue and engagement will serve to maintain forward momentum that builds upon achievements and to continue diffusing culture change through organisations and the system. For certain conversations, and as trust continues to develop, not everyone needs to be in the room. A regulator co-ordination group could enable movement on issues relevant to regulators in the water sector and help address the inevitable trade-offs that the sector faces as climate change and customer engagement become embedded in what Scottish Water does, allowing these parties to compare approaches and find common ground with the end goal of creating a lasting and systemic EBR environment. Such a group would limit resource use from other parties, and transparency of the outcomes of meetings will support trust even when decisions do not directly involve all parties. Involving other sectors and regulators over time in a dialogue on EBP and its practical implications can help create a common EBR-informed approach to regulation.

Box 1.3. Defining approaches for strategic public engagement in South Australia

A tailored engagement strategy helps regulators maintain high-quality participation even in the context of diverse needs and limited resources. Regulators have taken diverse approaches to providing clarity on the objectives of engagement efforts and expectations for participants.

The Essential Services Commission of South Australia (ESCOSA) maintains a Charter of Consultation and Regulatory Practice, updated every three years, that explains its approach to consulting and engaging with stakeholders. ESCOSA implements what it calls a "fit-for-purpose engagement", adapting its tools to meet needs. In each decision, ESCOSA recognises that appropriate levels of engagement depend on its "objective, outcomes, timeframes, resources and levels of concern or interest." It defines potential consultation approaches for different types of public commission outputs. For example, for draft decisions or determinations, ESCOSA's approach may include public forums, briefings with industry and targeted stakeholder meetings. Final decisions, on the other hand, would more likely be subject to an informational communiqué during industry briefings or stakeholder meetings.

This approach reflects the same underlying principle as the IAP2 spectrum of public participation – clear guidelines for public participation creates transparency about the regulators' goals and expectations for involvement.

Source: Essential Services Commission of South Australia (2019), Charter of consultation and regulatory practice, https://www.escosa.sa.gov.au/regulatory-approach/charter-of-consultation-and-regulatory-practice.

The outlook for the future: The next SRC

The next SRC provides an important opportunity to solidify the roles, methodologies and modalities that will also help guide the delivery of SRC21 as the SRC process becomes more continuous and takes a long-term perspective. One of the distinguishing features of the SRC21 was the development shared objectives and a clear vision on outcomes while experimenting with new ways of working. Experimentation resulted in the emerging role of the Stakeholder Advisory Group, the introduction of the EBR Review Group, and the transformation of the Customer Forum. Parties put fresh energies into "reinventing" the SRC. As the regulatory cycle becomes more continuous and seamless, there is an opportunity to take stock of what is already in place and what is needed in terms of groups, fora and advice. Participants should invest in codifying and documenting these roles and providing a roadmap for how to work together, building on the process, groups and mechanisms already put in place, that can serve as an input to the SRC27 methodology.

SRC21 benefited from having the 'right people in the room,' but future SRCs may not have this advantage. Many of the participants have been active in the sector throughout the previous regulatory period and started SRC21 with a high degree of familiarity with the regulation of the sector and with each other. The SRC21 process further strengthened relationships among participants, and some participants reported that a stakeholder group with strong relationships functioned better. However, as the composition of those in decision-making positions in the Scottish water sector changes over time, the replicability of the new approach taken in SRC21 will hinge on the ability of the framework to remain resilient to people changes. Participants are aware of the importance of succession planning, and participant institutions have already involved other individuals in SRC21 beyond the most familiar faces.

SRC21 aimed to transition the sector away from an adversarial approach to regulation, but it is important that professional, credible and robust challenge in future SRCs remains. SRC21 placed emphasis on moving away from an adversarial approach to regulation, which the regulator considered would increase opportunities and willingness to produce and share data and information and create opportunities for collaborative working. The delivery period should include ample opportunity for candid and open exchange, and embrace necessary tensions and opportunities for challenge. As WICS drafts its methodology for the next SRC, it would benefit from considering how the EBR-inspired approach can continue to offer benefits while allowing constructive debate and qualified challenge to thrive.

Recommendations

Starting planning for the next SRC now will allow parties to translate lessons learned to strengthen and streamline the upcoming process. Parties should discuss key parameters about the "who," "what" and "how" of SRC27. Early discussion can already set a "no surprises" tone for SRC27 and help parties identify areas where process efficiencies could be realised. Parties can consider developing a collective draft framework and approach document for the governance and process of SRC27 that documents perspectives of parties to build a common language and understanding going into SRC27.

Parties can build upon the experience of SRC21 to establish firmer expectations earlier in the SRC process. During SRC21, key outputs establishing the policy and regulatory parameters were delayed or revised. A higher level of trust and transparency within the participant group meant that progress continued without the timely codification of parameters. Changing core inputs and timelines also provided flexibility that enabled important developments, like the shift to a strategic plan. However, the early establishment of formal parameters can provide reassuring solidity to the framework within which participants act in future SRCs. In addition, formally defining key parameters early bolsters the external transparency of the proceedings.

Parties should consider how to harness stakeholder, customer, and community input and action for highest impact. WICS and other parties should evaluate the effectiveness of the ICG and other means to convey the views of customers and communities ahead of SRC27 to see the extent to which customers' and communities' views can be fully reflected in delivery and strategic thinking, such as bigger-picture issues. The usefulness of a separate body focused exclusively on the views of customers and communities should be weighed against the risk of overcrowding the landscape of actors already involved in the SRCs and the need for Scottish Water to fully integrate these views into its decision-making processes.

Box 1.4. Making the most of participatory processes in South Australia

The economic regulation of water and wastewater services in South Australia provides a range of avenues for engagement. Two bodies of customer representatives – the Negotiation Forum and the Consumer Experts Panel – provide customer challenge and feed customer views into processes for making regulatory determinations (revenue and service standard decisions) for the state-owned South Australian monopoly water provider, SA Water.

Negotiation Forum

ESCOSA established the Negotiation Forum to provide a challenge function during the development of the business plan that guides the future actions and investments of SA. The Negotiation Forum comprised an independent chair, a member of the Consumer Experts Panel (see below) and a member of SA Water's Customer Working Group (appointed by ESCOSA), meeting in session with senior executives from SA Water (including the CEO). An Independent Probity Advisor, also appointed by ESCOSA, oversaw the forum's activities.

The Negotiation Forum was intended to provide a vehicle for SA Water's planning and assumptions to be challenged through the development of the business plan, prior to that plan being submitted to ESCOSA for further public and regulatory review and scrutiny. The intended outcomes were that the resultant plan would be more capable of ready regulatory acceptance and, importantly, that SA Water would obtain the benefit arising from external – but not regulatory – challenges to its internal thinking and processes.

Consumer Experts Panel

A sitting panel comprised of representatives from two groups: ESCOSA's Consumer Advisory Committee and SA Water's customer advisory groups. ESCOSA's Consumer Advisory Committee – which includes representatives from consumers in water, sewerage, electricity and gas – advises the Commission regarding pricing, service standards, consumer protections, licensing and related regulatory issues. SA Water maintains its own customer advisory groups – one representing residential customers and the other representing business customers – that report directly to the SA Water board.

ESCOSA brought the two groups together, in joint sitting, to provide a vehicle for customers and customer groups to be able identify and flag issues important to them early in the regulatory decision-making process. The Panel produced a report, clearly setting out those issues, which was published and required SA Water to directly respond to it in its business plan. The Panel also had direct access to the Negotiation Forum – providing support and advice to the consumer members, enhancing their capacity to negotiate with SA Water throughout the regulatory process. ESCOSA also provided resources and support to allow the Panel to provide input, submissions and research to inform the regulatory determination. Together, these two groups allowed ESCOSA to better harness the expertise and perspectives of customer representatives in regulatory decision making.

Source: Essential Services Commission of South Australia (n.d.), Consumer Advisory Committee, https://www.escosa.sa.gov.au/regulatory-approach/consumer-advisory-committee; Essential Services Commission of South Australia (n.d.), Negotiation Forum, https://www.escosa.sa.gov.au/industry/water/retail-pricing/sa-water-regulatory-determination-2020/negotiation-forum; Essential Services Commission of South Australia (n.d.), SA Consumer Experts Panel, https://www.escosa.sa.gov.au/industry/water/retail-pricing/sa-water-regulatory-determination-2020/sa-consumers-expert-panel; SA Water (2014), Customer Engagement Program, https://www.sawater.com.au/__data/assets/pdf_file/0018/22644/SA-Water-Customer-Engagement-Program-Stage-1-Report.pdf; Information from ESCOSA, 2021.

Note

[1] The "stakeholder" group included a range of parties beyond WICS, Scottish Water and the Scottish Government, including the Drinking Water Quality Regulator, the Scottish Environment Protection Agency, Citizens Advice Scotland, and the Customer Forum for SRC21.

References

Hodges, C. (2016), *Ethical Business Regulation: Growing Empirical Evidence*, Policy Brief, The Foundation for Law, Justice and Society, https://www.fljs.org/sites/default/files/migrated/publications/Ethical%20Business%20Regulation.pdf (accessed on 6 May 2022). [2]

Hodges, C. and R. Steinholtz (2018), "The International Adoption of Ethical Business Regulation", *Policy Brief, The Foundation for Law, Justice and Society*, https://www.fljs.org/sites/default/files/migrated/publications/The%20International%20Adoption%20of%20Ethical%20Business%20Regulation.pdf (accessed on 6 May 2022). [3]

Scottish Government (2019), *Protecting Scotland's Future: the Government's Programme for Scotland 2019-2020*, https://www.gov.scot/publications/protecting-scotlands-future-governments-programme-scotland-2019-20/pages/5/. [1]

2 Context and background

Since the initial regulatory framework in Scotland was established in 1999, the economic regulation of the water sector in Scotland has evolved considerably to address changing objectives and involve new actors. This chapter provides an overview of the market structure of the sector, the actors involved in economic regulation, and the regulatory approach over time.

Market structure

Water and wastewater services in Scotland's household market are provided by Scottish Water, established in 2002. Scottish Water is the monopoly provider within the household market. In the non-household market, liberalised in 2008, Scottish Water's ring-fenced retail subsidiary Business Stream competes with other providers (Scottish Parliament, 2005[1]). Scottish Water is a public company with the Scottish Government as its sole shareholder. It replaced the three former regional water authorities in a move aimed at addressing systemic inefficiencies and providing harmonised charges across Scotland. These market arrangements for water and wastewater services differ from those that apply to the rest of the United Kingdom.[1]

Scottish Water provides water and wastewater wholesale and retail services to around 2.3 million domestic customer and wholesale services to around 140 000 businesses and public bodies. Scottish Water is fully funded by charges paid by its customers. It is also able to access appropriate borrowing from the Scottish Government.

The vast majority of households pay their water charges to their local councils, based on council (property) tax bands rather than on metered consumption. Household meters are limited to a small number of households that have requested and assumed certain installation costs to measure and bill based on consumption (Citizens Advice Scotland, 2021[2]). Charges are broadly cost-reflective between broad categories of customers (Hendry, 2016[3]) although there is undoubtedly cross-subsidy between urban and rural customers and across geographic areas. The average household bill was GBP 372 in 2020/2021, although there is considerable variation between the charges of the lowest and highest council tax bands (Scottish Water, 2020[4]). In the same financial year, Scottish Water's annual revenues were GBP 1 667 million. Scottish Water's net new borrowing during this year amounted to GBP 219 million and its capital programme is more than GBP 600 million per annum in current prices (Scottish Water, 2021[5]).

Key institutions

When determining the limits on charges that customers pay for Scottish Water services, the Scottish Government and WICS are key actors. The Scottish Government initiates each Strategic Review of Charges, providing the overarching principles and objectives that frame the SRC process. WICS, the economic regulator for water and wastewater services in Scotland, delivers a final determination that is in keeping with these Principles of Charging and Ministerial Objectives.

A number of Scottish institutions play a role in the price review process and the oversight of the sector. Water quality regulation and environmental regulation are performed by the Drinking Water Quality Regulator (DWQR) and the Scottish Environmental Protection Authority (SEPA). In addition, Citizens Advice Scotland (CAS) as the statutory body advising consumers plays an important consultative role in the price-setting process. While none of these bodies have a statutory role in price setting, all of these bodies have played an advisory role in SRC21. Their formal roles intersect with the economic regulation during the definition of needs and monitoring of delivery. They have a role in the development of the Ministerial Objectives (through a Scottish Government led process termed "Quality and Standards"). In addition, WICS, DWQR, SEPA and CAS work with the Scottish Government to monitor Scottish Water's delivery of the objectives and related outcomes, previously as part of an Output Monitoring Group which has been reformed as a Delivery Assurance Group for SRC21. These bodies' roles are summarised in Annex A.

An evolving regulatory approach in the Scottish water sector

The regulatory approach in the Scottish water sector has evolved over time from what was perceived as a more adversarial model to one seen as more collaborative, enabled by improvements in performance. Initial periods of adversarial and contested settlements were demanding and resource-intensive processes. Through successive price reviews, as information sharing and performance improved, the scope for disputes reduced and the adversarial nature of the process could evolve towards a more collaborative settlement. At the beginning of the journey, benchmarking analysis played an important role to promote efficiencies. However, the regulator observed that efficiency comparisons progressively became less effective, especially as performance indicators converged over time. With benchmarking no longer providing the same incentives, competition-like pressure needed to be exercised through different means.

In the case of Scotland, the regulatory "journey" has moved in stages, from:

- an initial position of maintaining a traditional regulatory distance with a degree of scepticism about drivers and performance;

- into a more adversarial and sceptical relationship caused by a perceived lack of progress in delivery and incomplete and at times inconsistent information which led to a lack of trust;

- then to an adversarial but more trusting relationship when robust information sharing was established and traditional regulatory tools could be employed, and;

- finally to a collaborative and trusting relationship where performance had improved to a point that the traditional regulatory tools had served their purpose and a new approach was required.

The regulatory process between 2002 and 2015

When the initial regulatory framework in Scotland was established in 1999, there were two clear challenges – to close the considerable efficiency gap with privatised companies in England and Wales, and to meet nationally and internationally required water quality and environmental standards. A regulatory framework featuring close monitoring and performance benchmarking, adapted from the regime for privatised water and sewerage companies in England and Wales, promised rapid and significant improvements in the newly-established Scottish Water. The framework soon gave way to one that closer resembles today's model, adding an independent Commission with the power to determine charges and develop incentive-based regulation.

This period marks the first use of enhanced consumer representation in the economic regulation of the water sector in Scotland. The independent organisation Waterwatch Scotland was established to represent customer views, with the ability to make complaints about water and wastewater providers. The organisation was short-lived; it disbanded in 2010 as part of the re-organisation of consumer representation in Scotland. The Scottish Public Services Ombudsman absorbed their complaints function, while Consumer Focus Scotland inherited their representation function. During the same period, WICS started to consult directly with stakeholders on the company's business plan, using consumer representative bodies' research as an input, and the draft determination, where groups served as statutory consultees.

Outcomes and limitations

During this period, the evolving regulatory framework accomplished its goals of improving Scottish Water performance. Scottish Water transformed itself as an organisation, catching up with the top performing companies in England and Wales on cost efficiency and levels of service. Since 2005, the company regularly reached – and outperformed – its targets. Charges increased at around the rate of inflation during this period, while customer service levels increased significantly.

In its thinking about the lessons for future price reviews, the economic regulator soon realised that its approach should evolve to reflect these improvements in performance and encourage quality stakeholder engagement. As the relationship between the regulator and Scottish Water increasingly allowed for exploring challenges through constructive dialogue, the regulator hoped to move away from the traditional "parent-child relationship" (WICS, 2013, p. 19[6]). WICS also acknowledged that highly technical stakeholder workshops were inaccessible to many customers and representatives, and that customers struggled to put WICS decisions and documents in context to understand impacts on their services or charges (WICS, 2013, p. 27[6]). Exiting this early phase of regulation, WICS identified the need for the regulator-company relationship to evolve and the need to facilitate meaningful consumer engagement.

The Strategic Review of Charges 2015-2021 (SRC15)

The regulatory approach in SRC15 would tackle these two needs head-on, allowing greater flexibility for the company's investment programmes and incorporating more substantial consumer inputs. The improvement in Scottish Water's financial performance, levels of service and compliance throughout previous reviews of charges enabled these changes. In addition, the company was approaching a regulatory plateau, meeting a relatively stable set of standards, in a relatively stable environment, with low inflation and minimal price increases. In this context, benchmarking improvements and benchmarking against English companies had limited usefulness (Littlechild, 2014[7]). Instead, as argued by Hendry (2016[8]), "identifying, and meeting, the wishes of customers becomes more important, around discretionary spend and around the phasing of improvements' (Hendry, 2016, p. 10[8]). To provide further challenge and exert further competitive pressure on Scottish Water, WICS introduced new changes in this regulatory period that offered flexibility in business plans and an enhanced customer voice in the process

The regulatory approach

WICS made a number of other significant changes to the regulatory approach ahead of SRC15, such as allowing greater flexibility and adopting a longer-term view. First, WICS abandoned the prescriptive framework used in the past in favour of a more flexible approach. The Commission did not provide detailed guidance and templates for Scottish Water to complete in its business planning, allowing the company to produce a more strategic, customer-oriented business plan (WICS, 2013, p. 22[6]). Second, WICS required Scottish Water to adopt a long-term view. It further extended the formal price review period from five to six years, and asked the company to draft a 25-year strategic vision document estimating the resources the company would need to achieve long-term objectives, with the expectation that Scottish Water's 6-year business plan would be aligned with the strategic vision. In parallel, the regulator saw the updated regulatory framework as an opportunity to provide assurance that Scottish Water would be financed sustainably in the interest of both current and future customers (WICS, 2013[6]). As part of their guidance, WICS therefore introduced a set of "financial tramlines"[2] to indicate to Scottish Water and its regulators whether it would be outperforming, or underperforming, in cash and capital value terms. The tramlines provided the possibility of "rebalancing" during the regulatory period while still reflecting the spirit of the agreement between the Customer Forum and the company (Littlechild, 2014, p. 15[7]).

Consumer engagement

WICS sought to elevate the voice of customers in the regulatory process, providing a strong alternative driver for improvements as technical benchmarking became less useful. Inspired by the UK Civil Aviation Authority (CAA) constructive engagement model and negotiated settlements in the United States and Canada, WICS solicited stakeholder and expert views on creating a new body to represent customers' views. While all stakeholders were supportive of the idea, each had their own reservations. Scottish Water was not fully convinced that it had to do more to legitimise its business plan – particularly as its reported performance had improved markedly. Scottish Ministers and Government officials worried about the legitimacy and representativeness of the proposed body. Consumer bodies were unclear about role allocation across policy and regulatory issues (Littlechild, 2014[7]).

Despite initial concerns, WICS, Scottish Water and the National Consumer Council reached an agreement to create the first "Customer Forum" and detailing the roles, timeline and composition of the group. This provided the necessary certainty that the newly established body would be an integral part of SRC15 and built confidence with stakeholders about the role of the Customer Forum. However, the Forum was created for the purpose of SRC15 only and without making any statutory changes to the regulatory process, in order to retain some flexibility and consolidate the progress made in previous SRCs.

The Forum's remit expanded from the role established in the formal agreement, and WICS's eventual expansion of its role demonstrated the dilution of the adversarial regulatory relationship between Scottish Water and WICS. The agreement gave the Forum the role of working with Scottish Water on a programme of research in order to establish customer priorities for service level improvements, understand and represent those priorities and preferences to WICS and Scottish Water, and ensure the most appropriate outcome for consumers based on those priorities and preferences. Soon, WICS formally expanded the Forum's role to include negotiating Scottish Water's entire business plan with the company. WICS shared its views on possible ranges for all of the key inputs before the Forum negotiated the business plan with the company. WICS did not formally commit to accepting or incorporating any agreement or views in its final determination (Littlechild, 2014, p. 6[7]) but did indicate that they would be minded to accept an agreement between Scottish Water and the Customer Forum that fell within the ranges that had been set.

The Forum's composition reflected the group's role as a conduit for customer views in the SRC based on evidence, rather than a representative group. It was charged with, among other attributions, "[u]nderstanding and representing to the Commission and to Scottish Water the priorities and preferences of customers (as a whole) in the SRC 2015-2020 process as identified through the customer research" (WICS, Scottish Water, and the National Consumer Council, 2011[9]). Led by a chair jointly appointed by the parties to the agreement, the group did not claim to be representative of household or business customers, consisting of five ordinary members with "strong customer focussed reputation", two ordinary members from the largest service providers in the country, and one ordinary member from the Scottish Council of Development and Industry. The chair received an annual sum commensurate with a commitment of 90 days per financial year and all other members committed to 50 days per financial year, funded by WICS.

A negotiating team from the Forum and Scottish Water entered into a Minute of Agreement in 2014, building upon an iterative process of negotiations in previous years. Informed by WICS's notes and research, the Forum and Scottish Water began to agree on a number of priorities around service quality levels, investment and customer service throughout 2012 and 2013. Scottish Water published its long-term strategic projections in October 2013. There was some involvement of SEPA and DWQR in providing clarification around quality requirements and the budgets needed to achieve those requirements. When the Forum and the company signed the Minute of Agreement after twelve hours of negotiation, it marked the Forum's approval of Scottish Water's business plan for 2015-2021. WICS adopted a determination consistent with the Minute of Agreement, formalising its acceptance of the result of negotiations.

Box 2.1. The role of consultative bodies in the regulatory decision-making process at Portugal's Energy Services Regulatory Authority (ERSE)

ERSE's Statutes form the foundation for the regulator's inclusive and transparent decision-making approach, through the creation of three consultative bodies (known as councils), which contribute to the development of its technical regulations, tariff decisions and the broad lines of action and deliberations

---

taken by ERSE's Board of Directors. The three consultative councils – Advisory Council, Tariff Council and Fuels Council – act as a forum for creating consensus among key stakeholders.

As part of a broader consultation and engagement policy, the councils issue non-binding opinions on ERSE's regulatory proposals. Importantly, where the regulator does not take on board the opinions presented by the councils, it must justify in writing why it has not adopted the council's proposed changes. Together with ERSE's other engagement mechanisms, this process ensures accountability and strengthens the integrity of the regulator's decisions. In addition, they provide a permanent platform for stakeholders to meet and understand each other's perspectives. In this way, the councils provide stability to stakeholders and achieve consensus in their statements in an impressive 90% of cases.

The councils are composed of a broad spectrum of representation from national, regional and municipal government, consumer organisations and the energy industry. Council members serve a non-remunerated and renewable term of three years. Each council decides how often to meet in order to prepare its opinions. Generally speaking, and in response to the increased activities and responsibilities of the regulator, the councils may meet several times a month. All opinions of the councils are approved by majority vote, although if members do not agree with all or parts of the opinion of the council they can state this in the submission to ERSE. The opinions of the councils are made public and published on the ERSE website.

More specifically, as regards tariffs and prices, in line with a timeline fixed by law, ERSE must submit its draft proposals to the Tariff Council, which delivers non-binding opinions on the review and approval of the tariff codes, as well as on the annual determination of tariffs and prices. The plenary and sectoral sections of the Tariff Council (electricity section and natural gas section) are chaired by a person of recognised standing and independence appointed by the member of the Government responsible for energy.

Given the characteristic asymmetry of information and resources between the industry and consumers, ERSE seeks to facilitate the latter's engagement in a number of ways. First, industry and consumer representatives must be represented in equal numbers. Second, ERSE provides a subsistence and attendance allowance for consumer representatives, as well as for government, public bodies and representatives from Azores and Madeira. In addition, ERSE provides training to the household consumer associations that sit on its consultative councils in order to build their capacity and ability to contribute to deliberations.

Source: Information provided by ERSE, 2022.

Key outcomes of an evolving regulatory process

The more flexible, customer-centric approach to water regulation in SRC15 has been praised as one of the most "innovative, successful and encouraging developments in UK utility regulation" (Littlechild, 2014, p. 1[7]). The *ex post* reviews undertaken and the feedback collected from industry stakeholders highlight that:

- By being asked to negotiate the business plan with the provider, the Customer Forum was delegated real power from the economic regulator, which however retained the position of final arbiter and contributed to the final settlement by providing key guidance and technical information to the Forum.

- Scottish Water's understanding of what customers want appears to have improved, thanks to the new framework pushing the company to assess customer needs more in-depth and to provide a more careful examination of the rationale for its investment plans.

- Negotiated prices were perhaps lower than they would have been under a traditional regulatory framework; in exchange for this concession, Scottish Water was able to plan future investment and operations earlier on by reaching a timely agreement and to embed elements of flexibility in its business planning.

Institutional innovation: The Customer Forum

The introduction of the Forum changed the roles and approaches of both WICS and Scottish Water during SRC15. To provide the necessary inputs for the Forum, WICS had to adopt a more strategic role in setting expectations around a number of parameters and assumptions very early on in the process. Its analytical focus shifted accordingly from somewhat static assessments of efficiency to more forward-looking analyses of high-level challenges. Those higher expectations have influenced Scottish Water, encouraging the company to better understand what customers want and pushing it to think more carefully about the rationale for its investment.

The new regulatory framework gave a prominent role and operational freedom to the Forum, while clearly defining the parameters within which the Forum could negotiate with Scottish Water to agree upon a business plan. While these processes placed restrictions on the negotiation, the Forum still had the opportunity to challenge and test the views of both the regulator on the ranges for key parameters and the company on assumptions for setting charges and prioritising investment. While the Forum conducted only limited customer research, it showed some ability to interpret research inputs critically and prompt some research into customer views.

Moreover, Forum members gained WICS's support to negotiate the entire business plan with Scottish Water while not having any obligation to find an agreement and knowing that WICS would be the "decision-maker of last resort". As a result, they felt empowered to exert pressure on a wide range of issues within the designated "safe space" in the framework. It is worth noting that "the operational freedom that the Forum seized as an opportunity could well have turned into a weakness, as it could have resulted in lack of focus and poor effectiveness". In fact, "some members had some initial misgivings about the absence of a clear direction of travel or detailed process" (Customer Forum, 2015, p. 22[10]).

A legacy report recording observations from the first Forum also recognises that the consumer engagement and regulatory approach to SRC15 further contributed to a shift away from the adversarial nature of the price determination and towards a more accessible model. It presented a more constructive approach aimed at "finding acceptable compromise", putting the customer "at the heart of the decision-making process", and increasing the transparency of decision making by making Scottish Water's documents (including the business plan) more accessible to a non-technical audience (Customer Forum, 2015[10]). Littlechild (2014[7]) notes that the regulatory documents are more understandable, more accessible and substantially shorter than in previous SRCs.

These positive outcomes did not come about without obstacles. Some of the Board members in the Commission initially felt uneasy about the perceived delegation of statutory responsibilities from the regulator to the Forum and they maintained some reservations during the discussions about the future of the Forum post SRC15. Within Scottish Water, the CEO and senior management were heavily involved in gaining internal buy-in for this new approach in light of the perceived benefits to the way the company operated.

Customer views at the centre of the Final Determination of Charges

Stakeholders in the Scottish water industry agree that the new process was instrumental in driving a far greater focus on customers, reflected in the parameters and commitments contained in the Final Determination of Charges adopted by WICS.

New parameters

Exchanges between the Customer Forum and Scottish Water led to an agreement that sketched the trajectory of charges over the regulatory period. The negotiation of charges for the six-year period 2015-2021 was influenced by the Forum's research on the impact of the economic crisis on affordability and the need to keep prices low in light of decreasing real incomes. The final determination fixed an upper limit for Scottish Water's charges over the entire period, setting the overall tariff cap for household customers over the six-year regulatory period was set at no more than CPI minus 1.8%. It established a cap in nominal prices over the first years of the regulatory period, and allowed increases for remaining years relative to inflation. For the non-household market, WICS decided to freeze default tariffs for non-household customers in nominal terms for six years.

The parties agreed a price cap in constant nominal prices (irrespective of inflation) for the last year of the previous regulatory control period and the first three years of the 2015-2021 period. For this period, charges were set to increase by 1.6% per year in nominal terms. The nominal value was chosen with the intent to provide greater certainty to customers and better transparency as to what the price increases would mean. In this instance Scottish Water accepted a higher risk, however, in the context of a low inflation environment.

The regulator would still establish price increases for the remaining years in the regulatory period relative to inflation. This time, the regulator and the Government agreed to use CPI (consumer price index) instead of RPI (retail price index). The former is a measure that is more closely aligned to the perception that consumers have of price trends in the economy and is more easily understood. For the following three-year period, prices would rise at CPI minus 0.3%, subject to the overall requirement.

In addition, the Customer Forum agreed "a higher level of capital efficiency with Scottish Water than the economic regulator could have required using available benchmarking techniques". In this respect, the Forum's key message was that if the company carried any inefficiency, customers would not pay for it. The Forum's scrutiny of the rationale for investment programmes resulted in Scottish Water having to justify and reassess its investment propositions in more detail than was previously the case, finding ways to meet objectives in manners that are more efficient (WICS, 2014[11]).

New approaches to innovation

WICS also introduced changes aimed at encouraging the use of innovative solutions. First, WICS allowed Scottish Water to factor in costs of any additional risk to the underlying cost of meeting a defined outcome. This measure was based on the recognition that innovation will inevitably result in some failures. By allowing an additional provision for risk, Scottish Water would be given the resources to resort to more traditional solutions in case of failure. To take up this risk-adjusted cost approach, Scottish Water would have to demonstrate that the total cost of the portfolio of projects (including the costs of the risk adjustment) would be lower than that of the next best alternative (WICS, 2017[12]). Scottish Water and the Customer Forum agreed to ring-fence the additional risk allowance in a "risk reserve" to ensure that Scottish Water always had the cash resources it may require to deliver the required outputs efficiently and effectively.

New performance measures

Three new performance measures were developed by Scottish Water and the Customer Forum for introduction in the six-year period 2015-2021. As described in the Final Determination (WICS 2013), these measures are:

- the household customer experience measure;
- the non-household customer experience measure; and
- the "high esteem" test.

Similar to the Service Incentive Mechanism developed by Ofwat in England and Wales, the household customer experience measure is built from a quantitative and a qualitative component. The new measure is also the first performance measure to include the views of customers who have experienced an issue with their service but did not make direct contact with Scottish Water.

A similar measure is also being developed for non-household customers. These will help customers and other stakeholders to compare the service that is provided by Scottish Water year on year and, potentially, with services provided by other water and sewerage companies.

The high esteem test is used to compare Scottish Water's reputation among the public with those of other UK utilities,[3] and also with the country's most trusted companies and brands across all sectors.

The key areas of focus going into SRC21

SRC15 had started a paradigm shift that would put a clear onus on Scottish Water to take ownership and demonstrate that it is focused on delivering for customers. This paradigm shift also brought to the fore a number of areas that would need to be developed further in the SRC21 and on which WICS started reflecting in preparation for SRC21.

The overall issue of asset maintenance and replacement had been an underlying theme SRC15. Innovative measures had been introduced to ensure that resources would be appropriately set aside and used to ensure that quality water would continue to "run through the tap". However, there was also the realisation that Scottish Water might not yet have all the necessary capabilities to make the best informed decisions on the state of the assets. Scottish Water's ownership would also mean a shift in the organisational culture of Scottish Water, including in being proactive in identifying and alerting on current and future risks.

SRC15 had put a strong focus on eliciting the views of customers and ensure that these views were reflected in regulatory decisions. The Customer Forum had been one of the conduits of these views. The Forum was reinstated and set up earlier than for SRC15 with a partly renewed composition. Half of the previous members (including the Chair) were retained to guarantee some experience and continuity. The balance between members drawn from the wider public and from the water industry was marginally shifted towards business customers (water providers Business Stream, Anglian Water and Veolia each have a member on the Forum). Members of the public were selected through an open tender procedure managed by the Consumer Futures Unit of Citizens Advice Scotland. WICS also provided the Forum with a larger budget for SRC21 compared with SRC15. WICS also tried to support the use of innovative methods to elicit the "true" preferences of customers, including by exploring the use of behavioural sciences. This effort would lead to establishing a research coordination group between the Customer Forum, Consumer Futures Unit and Scottish Water (with WICS and the Scottish Government as observers) to coordinate research efforts and share outputs as they emerge.

Finally, to facilitate a shift towards open collaboration in line with the principles of ethical business regulation, WICS also started thinking of ways to facilitate continuous dialogue among all stakeholders from the beginning of the process. Starting as informal meetings triggered by the first OECD peer review of SRC21, these meetings evolved into joint stakeholder meetings with all actors in the Scottish water sector, to take place regularly throughout the process.

As the SRC21 unfolded, a number of challenges emerged that informed the process and partly determined its outcome. These key challenges with the way in which they were initially addressed and how they evolved throughout the process will be discussed in the following section.

Notes

[1] The Water Act 1989 privatised the water industry in England and Wales.

[2] For a detailed description of financial tramlines see WICS 2017a, pp. 67-69

[3] Based on the UK Customer Satisfaction Index (CSI). More details at:
https://www.instituteofcustomerservice.com/research-insight/uk-customer-satisfaction-index.

References

Citizens Advice Scotland (2021), *Water Meters*,
   https://www.citizensadvice.org.uk/scotland/consumer/water/water-and-sewerage-s/water-meters-s/ (accessed on 30 July 2021). [2]

Customer Forum (2015), *Legacy Report*. [10]

Hendry, S. (2016), "Scottish Water: a public-sector success story", *Water International*, Vol. 41/6, pp. 900-915, https://doi.org/10.1080/02508060.2016.1212961. [3]

Hendry, S. (2016), "The customer forum - Putting customers at the centre of regulating water services", *Water Policy*, Vol. 18/4, pp. 948-963, https://doi.org/10.2166/wp.2016.199. [8]

Littlechild, S. (2014), *The Customer Forum: customer engagement in the Scottish water sector*, https://www.eprg.group.cam.ac.uk/wp-content/uploads/2014/07/The-Customer-Forum-paper-11-July-2014.doc. [7]

Scottish Parliament (2005), *Water Services (Scotland) Act 2005*, https://www.legislation.gov.uk/asp/2005/3/pdfs/asp_20050003_en.pdf (accessed on 24 September 2020). [1]

Scottish Water (2021), *Annual Report & Accounts 2020/2021: Performance and Prospects*, https://www.scottishwater.co.uk/help-and-resources/document-hub/key-publications/annual-reports (accessed on 12 October 2021). [5]

Scottish Water (2020), *About Your Charges 2020-2021*, https://www.scottishwater.co.uk/Your-Home/Your-Charges/Your-Charges-2020-2021 (accessed on 12 October 2021). [4]

WICS (2017), *Innovation and Collaboration: future proofing the water industry for customers*. [12]

WICS (2014), *The Strategic Review of Charges 2015-21: Final Determination*, https://www.watercommission.co.uk/UserFiles/Documents/Final%20Determination%20-%20Final.pdf. [11]

WICS (2013), *Innovation and choice*, https://www.yumpu.com/en/document/view/35033600/innovation-and-choice-water-industry-commission-for-scotland. [6]

WICS, Scottish Water, and the National Consumer Council (2011), *Co-operation agreement establishing the Customer Forum for SRC 2015*, https://www.watercommission.co.uk/UserFiles/Documents/11102011%20-%20Cooperation%20agreement%20WICS%20SW%20CF.pdf. [9]

3 Overcoming key regulatory challenges

During SRC21, WICS and other parties aimed to modify the approach to economic regulation in the sector to address a range of interrelated challenges: 1) the limitations of an adversarial approach, 2) challenges associated with long-life assets and time inconsistency, 3) lack of flexibility of investment, and 4) embedding the customer and community voice. This chapter summarises and analyses the components and major milestones of SRC21 within each of these four challenges. Each of the sections summarises the starting point at the outset of SRC21, explores how WICS and stakeholders made progress within this area, and looks ahead towards emerging challenges.

Limitations of an adversarial approach

The starting point: balancing efficiency against the need to address long-term challenges

Looking back at the different SRCs, WICS considered that a regulatory approach based on the use of a "hard budget constraint" to ensure efficient outcomes was reaching its limits. The hard budget constraint is a common tool in the kit of economic regulators that set prices in network sectors, whereby the regulator sets the constraint at a level that is just sufficient to deliver the expenditure required to attain certain levels of service, if the regulated entities are efficient enough. This approach had ensured that the regulated utility had sufficient resources to meet efficiency targets and deliver the desired level of service within the given regulatory period. However, this focus on the efficient use of resources over a regulatory period of six years did not provide sufficient incentives to think long-term about the state of the assets and necessary repair, refurbishment and replacement, as well as the net-zero target. In WICS's view, traditional incentive regulation featuring a hard budget constraint was no longer delivering adequate results for customers.

WICS considered that the hard budget constraint had outlived its usefulness for a second reason: the adversarial relationship between regulator and regulated entity that this approach encouraged. WICS's Chief Executive observed that in his experience a more adversarial relationship could contribute further to asymmetry of information, and, in turn, the difficulty of the regulator's decision making. The adversarial nature can quickly become positively reinforced, as the regulator has to revert to tools like commissioning external reviews to reduce the effects of information asymmetries, which can further strain the relationship between regulator and company (Sutherland, 2021[1]).

WICS's efforts to reduce the adversarial nature of economic regulation in the Scottish water sector would build upon progress made in previous years. Following its establishment, WICS's 2006-10 price review was marked by a disagreement on the finances necessary to deliver the objectives set by the Scottish Ministers between the regulator and the company. Hendry (2016[2]) notes that the relationship between Scottish Water and WICS contributed to the failure to agree a business plan, which led subsequently to the resignation of the Scottish Water chair in 2006 (p. 952[2]). Since that time, both the regulator and company have focused on building a collaborative approach and, as a result, the reviews have become significantly less adversarial. Part of the evolution of this more collaborative approach was the development of a new body of specially-selected qualified individuals – the Customer Forum – that added a new dimension to the traditional bilateral relationship between regulator and company. The issue remained that the company was still primarily focused on what the regulator wanted, rather than taking ownership of its relationship with customers and the communities it serves.

As WICS prepared for SRC21, it aimed to build upon previous developments to further de-emphasise adversarial approaches by finding an alternative to a hard budget constraint and give greater ownership to Scottish Water through an open and candid dialogue on needs, priorities and constraints. Such an approach would need to ensure that the regulated entity would use resources set aside to finance long-term maintenance and replacement needs efficiently while enabling the company to attain the net-zero target. In addition, the approach would involve mechanisms to help the parties move further away from adversarial regulation.

Going into SRC21, WICS envisioned an approach based on building trust and fostering collaboration that would facilitate an open and transparent dialogue on the priorities for the sectors that would then serve as a basis for the sometimes-hard choices on where to put resources. The "hard budget constraint" would ultimately be replaced by a shared view on what to do, minimising the need and opportunities for hiding information and rather creating incentives to have an even better view of the challenges for the water sector.

The regulator took inspiration from ethical business regulation (EBR) and ethical business practice (EBP) (see Box 3.1). In the document establishing its methodology for SRC21, WICS described its motivations for shifting from a more traditional approach to economic regulation to an EBR/EBP approach, an idea that was influencing WICS's thinking even before the start of SRC21 with the introduction of the Customer Forum in SRC15. While the traditional approach delivered significant benefits in terms of sector outcomes, WICS expressed doubt that the traditional approach could continue to be as effective in the face of evolving and complex modern challenges including "increased uncertainty, the need to involve multiple stakeholders in identifying sustainable solutions and the timing of required expenditure" (WICS, 2017[3]). WICS explained that an EBR approach meant that the regulator would no longer rely solely on its powers of discipline, placing these functions on "stand-by mode" (WICS, 2020[4]). In turn, WICS expected Scottish Water to mainstream EBP, reflecting principles of ethical behaviour, openness and trust.

Box 3.1. EBR and EBP: Ethics in purpose and in process

When defining the concepts of EBR and EBP, the researchers that coined the terms start with EBP. EBP turns towards the entities involved in regulation themselves, establishing an expectation of ethical and fair behaviour by these parties. Hodges and Steinholtz (2017[5]) define EBP as "[a]n organisation in which the leaders consciously and consistently strive to create an effective ethical culture where employees do the right thing, based upon ethical values and supported by cultural norms and formal institutions." The researchers present EBP as a pre-condition for EBR, which is "[a] relationship between a business, or a group of businesses, and a regulator, or group of regulators, in which the business produces evidence of its ongoing commitment to EBP and the regulator recognises and encourages that commitment." EBR involves a commitment and a shift away from blame culture in regulation towards a culture based on openness and trust.

The concepts of EBR and EBP are multifaceted, but one concept at the heart of the EBR regulatory delivery model is self-assurance by the regulated company. In this case, an EBR approach would establish an expectation that Scottish Water should be able to find the best way to reassure stakeholders that they are meeting their legal responsibilities and beyond. It involves an expectation that the company reports its performance and prospects regularly and transparently, setting out what it will achieve in the short-, medium- and long-term. In this model, "the role of regulators should be mainly to provide information and advice to ensure that organisations assure themselves effectively and reliably, and intervene when they do not" (Hodges and Steinholtz, 2017[5]).

WICS defined expectations for how Scottish Water would embody EBP in its final determination. According to WICS, Scottish Water should:

- take full ownership of enduring relationships with the customers and communities it serves;
- promote an open discussion of its purpose, aspirations and values;
- set out clearly – and in a way that is accessible to all – its current performance and plans for improvement;
- engage in regular and frank discussion of performance, recognising that performance expectations will always change and become more demanding;
- adopt a collaborative, timely and pro-active approach to meeting the needs and aspirations of its regulators, aiming to address their concerns even before they have had to ask; and
- embrace these challenges as an opportunity – and be seen to do so in a positive and constructive way (WICS, 2020, p. 16[6]).

Furthermore, WICS saw alignment between the concept of EBP and evolving ideas of corporate purpose. It cites Colin Mayer, who argues that corporations should "produce profitable solutions to the

> problems of people and planet and not profit from producing problems for people and planet" (Mayer, 2018[7]; WICS, 2020[4]). This concept holds particular resonance in the Scottish water sector, with its publicly owned service provider.
>
> Source: (Hodges and Steinholtz, 2017[5]), Ethical Business Practice and Regulation: A Behavioural and Values-Based Approach to Compliance and Enforcement, Hart Publishing, Oxford, https://www.bloomsburyprofessional.com/uk/ethical-business-practice-and-regulation-9781509916368/ (accessed 23 March 2021); (Mayer, 2018[7]), Editorial: Averting corporate crises. British Academy Review, 3-5, retrieved from https://www.thebritishacademy.ac.uk/documents/348/BAR34-02-Mayer-Editorial.pdf (accessed on 23 March 2021).

This approach was a significant change compared to previous SRCs, including the last SRC that already introduced some important new features in the process. EBR and EBP have mostly developed as academic hypotheses rather than a practical methodology to regulate a sector. The novelty in applying these principles and approach has required some degree of experimentation and "trial and error" throughout the process. The following sections present the new elements introduced in SRC21 to support a shift away from the adversarial approach by embracing a new regulatory approach that seeks to mainstream EBR and EBP. It explains how the governance of the process created new opportunities for exchange, describing how collaborative processes furthered Scottish Water's Strategic Plan and the water sector vision. It presents a support group convened to perform a "temperature check" of EBR values in the process. Finally, it highlights the challenges posed by this new approach and how these challenges were addressed.

Moving ahead: SRC21 structures shift away from the adversarial approach

This new approach implied a shift from previous SRCs in which bilateral conversations and unilateral research were the norm. Stakeholders committed to a process bringing together regulators, stakeholders and businesses under a shared ethical framework emphasising trust and collaboration. SRC21 convened regular, formalised meetings of key stakeholders (first as Joint Stakeholder Meetings and later as the Stakeholder Advisory Group, or SAG) with working groups to consider specific issues within the regulatory process. Information-collecting processes within SRC21 became collaborative efforts. Decision making on many issues and some products also involved collaboration.

The multi-lateral governance of SRC21 creates new opportunity for exchange

Throughout the SRC, regular meetings of stakeholders brought together senior representatives of each stakeholder organisation: Scottish Government, WICS, Scottish Water, the Customer Forum, SEPA, DWQR and CAS. The OECD Secretariat was invited as an observer, and experts have been called to present ad hoc. The stakeholder group became a critical forum for advancing decision making, and also for the sharing of information and knowledge. For example, Scottish Water held a series of "deep dive" sessions to stakeholders to help all parties understand how the company operates.

The frequency of meetings increased to extract more value from these opportunities for exchange. Initially, the stakeholder group planned to convene every six months, as WICS agreed to promote both better communication and increased co-operation among stakeholders throughout the SRC. Soon it became apparent that these meetings brought significant benefits to the process, not least the ability to address crosscutting challenges in a transparent manner and profit from opportunities for mutual learning. To take advantage of the benefits of these meetings, more frequent, quarterly meetings were held throughout 2017-18. In the last quarter of 2018, WICS-chaired Joint Stakeholder Meetings occurred every month to enable faster progress. The meetings continued monthly thereafter.

The governance of these meetings shifted during 2018, when the WICS-chaired Joint Stakeholder Meetings became the Scottish Water-led SAG. Scottish Water took ownership of the SAG for the purpose of co-creating its Strategic Plan with stakeholders. In parallel, Scottish Water established six multilateral working groups where stakeholders provided input on key elements of its Strategic Plan and remaining parameters of SRC21. These working groups, each chaired by a Scottish Water employee, operated under terms of reference to produce an output or work towards a goal. The working groups reported to the SAG regularly, which in turn provides input on the working groups' progress. Scottish Water and WICS provided a joint programme management function, helping co-ordinate groups where necessary and maintaining a shared online repository for materials relevant to the SRC21 process. Towards the end of 2019, a representative from the Government helped co-ordinate the SRC as well as the Investment Planning and Prioritisation Group. This structure is pictured in Figure 3.1 below.

Figure 3.1. SRC21 governance structure

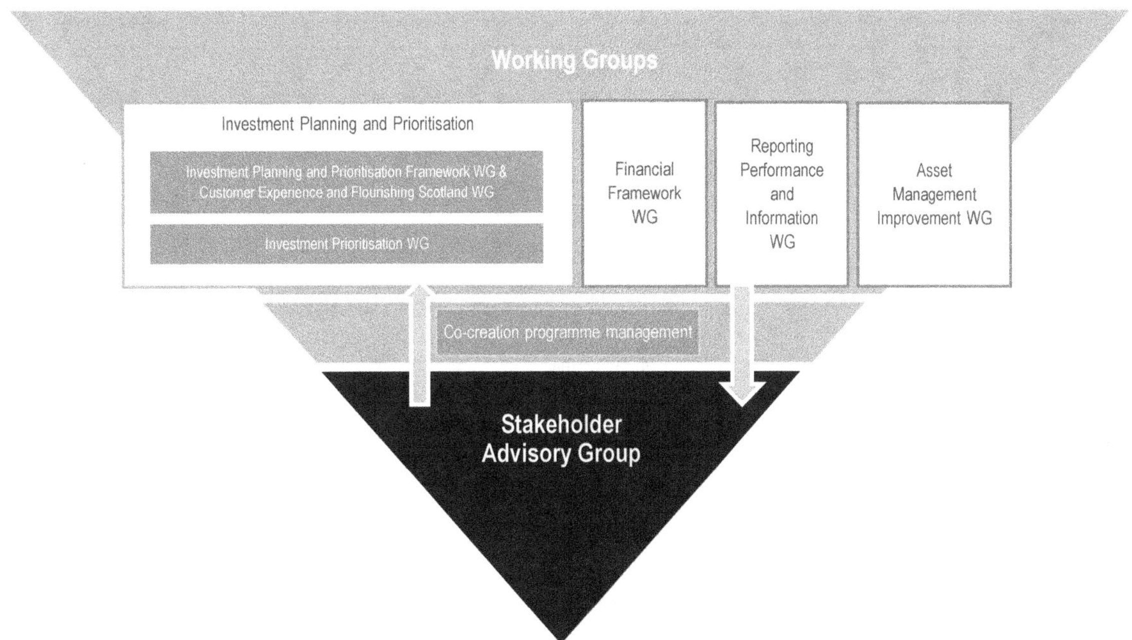

Source: Modified from the "SR21 Co-creation Approach" diagram presented by Scottish Water to the Stakeholder Advisory Group on 22 November 2018.

Stakeholders experiment with co-creation for Scottish Water's Strategic Plan and a sector vision

The idea of co-creating key outputs of SRC21 appealed to the stakeholder group, but the process was not well defined. After an early try to define principles for co-creation, Scottish Water's Strategic Plan represented a first attempt at co-creation. However, the process ultimately resembled something closer to joint review. A more advanced form of co-creation is exemplified in the sector vision, where stakeholders came together to create the vision from a blank page.

Scottish Water's Strategic Plan was the deliverable of central concern at many of the monthly stakeholder meetings, and the role of the stakeholder group in contributing to the Strategic Plan was established in a process that was more organic than premeditated. The proposal to use a "co-creation" process to create the Strategic Plan originated with Scottish Water, and WICS welcomed the proposal and extended the timeline for intermediate deliverables in order to provide adequate time for the process. The approach to the Strategic Plan first took shape in a series of letters exchanged between the CEO of WICS and the CEO of Scottish Water in September and October 2018. They agreed that the company would work collaboratively with its owner (the Scottish Government), its customers and its other stakeholders to co-create a Strategic Plan. The letter exchanges also outlined the approach to co-creating the Strategic Plan as one based on openness and transparency, in line with EBR principles.

Further procedural guidance came in the form of a set of principles establishing key parameters and norms for the co-creation process. Scottish Water created the Guiding Principles for co-creation of its Strategic Plan in November 2018. The principles expressed many of the characteristics stakeholders have come to associate with an ethical process: clearly identified roles, established avenues for influence, transparency, and standards for behaviour (Table 3.1). The stakeholder group discussed the principles at length, although the group stopped short of adopting the principles formally. Nevertheless, these principles and the discussions held about them provided a foundational shared understanding of some norms.

Table 3.1. Guiding principles for co-creation proposed by Scottish Water

Roles	<ul><li>Ministers Objectives have primacy</li><li>SW own the plan and produce outline</li><li>Respect regulatory and customer independence ensuring ongoing roles and duties are not compromised</li><li>This is a voluntary process – all stakeholders see benefit of staying the "in the raft"</li><li>Enables wider stakeholder discussions as appropriate</li></ul>
Influence	<ul><li>Everyone has proportionate input relevant to their remit and can see their impact.</li><li>Early engagement – not tinkering round edges at the end</li><li>Balancing both short term and long term considerations</li></ul>
Openness & Transparency	<ul><li>Share knowledge, expertise, insight and level of understanding</li><li>Accepting of need for bi-laterals that explore not decide</li><li>Multi-lateral when committing to positions that may utilise significant resource</li><li>Collective vision</li><li>Willingness to test ideas, not polished product</li><li>Open and questioning</li><li>Clear and honest about quality of evidence</li></ul>
Behaviours & Conduct	<ul><li>Willingness to consider different views - tension and challenge is explored and positively tackled</li><li>Candid and no blame culture</li><li>Trust, value and respect colleagues</li><li>Positive attitude</li></ul>
Practical & Usable	<ul><li>Recognises reality of stakeholder resource availability and tailors level of co-created product accordingly</li><li>Recognise that process goes beyond the Strategic Plan, particularly through the IPPF</li></ul>

Source: Scottish Water, Presentation to the 22 November 2018 Stakeholder Advisory Group meeting.

In practice, the iterative process of engaging stakeholders in the Strategic Plan creation fell short of complete co-creation. The process to draft the Strategic Plan involved group discussions, bilateral meetings, and informal presentations of draft documents as well as formal consultation processes. Many of these mechanisms did not lend themselves to co-creation; instead, Scottish Water would often advance separately (often with WICS or other organisations) and present new documents to the wider group.

The group also questioned whether an integral process of co-creation was desirable. Indeed, "co-creation" raised questions of who would "own" the final product, and whether decisions should be reached by consensus by all parties (which threatened to stretch beyond the statutory mandates of some stakeholders). While the entire process may not have been "co-creation," it was guided by EBR principles such as openness, a no-blame culture and transparency. This approach created a unique process that ramped up exchange between WICS, Scottish Water and stakeholders considerably.

Although much of the Strategic Plan process closer resembled joint review than co-creation, true co-creation took shape in the development of a sector vision. Stakeholders came together in a daylong workshop that took stakeholders through a series of exercises designed to elicit blue-sky visions of the sector, roadblocks impeding progress, and realistic goals for the sector. Scottish Water and the Customer Forum synthesised stakeholder input into drafts, further soliciting input from the group and from individual stakeholder organisations to maintain alignment. The final product (shown in Box 3.2), was jointly owned by all stakeholders. Stakeholders agree that the shared vision for the Scottish water industry was a successful result and a step towards co-creation (The Water Report, 2019[8]).

Box 3.2. A vision for the Scottish water sector, owned by stakeholders

A sweeping vision for the sector

The vision links performance to sustainability and Scottish policy, opening with "Scotland's water sector will be admired for excellence, secure a sustainable future and inspire a Hydro Nation." It touches upon water quality, environmental protection, economic prosperity, and affordability. Additionally, it expresses the sector's goal to strive for agility and resilience through collaboration within and beyond the sector.

The vision was conceived as a touchstone for the process going forward: notably, the vision should drive Scottish Water's Strategic Plan objectives.

Political buy-in supports the vision

After stakeholders launched the process to create a shared sector vision, the Cabinet Secretary for Environment, Climate Change and Land Reform formally called upon the stakeholders to create a vision for achievements in the sector over the next thirty years.

Ministers published the vision in the final Ministerial Objectives and Principles of Charging, giving it legal status.

Source: The Water Report (2019), Scotland's water sector co-creates vision with social purpose, https://www.thewaterreport.co.uk/single-post/2019/10/20/scotland-s-water-sector-co-creates-vision-with-social-purpose; Scottish Government (2020), Investing in and paying for water services: consultation, https://www.gov.scot/publications/investing-paying-water-services-2021-final-consultation/pages/3/.

The EBR support group offers a periodic "temperature check" of the SRC21 process

Stakeholders discussed the idea of an external form of assurance to accompany a transition towards EBR and EBP and, over time, the idea of an **EBR Support Group** (EBRSG) emerged. WICS's updated methodology issued in November 2018 formalised the creation of the EBRSG. The EBRSG would provide a regular "temperature-check" of trust, ownership, collaboration and openness by seeking stakeholders' perceptions at regular intervals and debriefing them on their findings. Agreeing to create the EBRSG was a key step in the direction of embedding EBR in SRC21 and a testament to stakeholders' willingness to reflect upon the degree of trust of the process as it happened.

The ways of working of the EBRSG allowed it to collect periodic, anonymous feedback from parties to reflect back to the stakeholder group. The EBRSG was tasked with assessing the SRC21 process on four dimensions: common understanding of the EBR framework, openness and transparency, reciprocal trust, and involvement and collaboration. The EBRSG conducted assessments via regular anonymous online surveys and face-to-face interviews. The survey used mainly closed-ended questions to capture participant views on their own role, the behaviour of stakeholder organisations and the functioning of the SRC21 system. The face-to-face interviews, lasting less than one hour each, allowed interviewers to explore the issues raised in the survey in more depth and ensure that respondents have interpreted the survey questions correctly. After each assessment, the EBRSG provided their analysis of the results of surveys and interviews to stakeholders along with recommendations and questions for consideration.

Through six assessments, conducted between 2019 and 2021, the EBRSG showed evolving stakeholder perceptions of the use of EBR principles in SRC21. The focus of stakeholders developed in response as the focus of the SRC21 process shifted, as summarised below:

- **Early assessments** showed an emphasis on operationalising EBR principles within the SRC process, increasing transparency within the SRC process and subsequently transparent communication to the public. They highlighted continued room for improvement in the SRC21 ways of working, suggesting that the group further clarify co-creation and roles, improve reception to constructive challenge, communicate clearly about bilateral meetings and reconsider resource demands for stakeholders. They also expressed early visions for the use of EBR/EBP going forward, with the group recommending that investment prioritisation is transparent and considering external communication about the SRC21 process.

- **As the content of the SRC shifted from agreeing key outputs to the phase of delivery**, stakeholders expressed uncertainty about the practicalities of future Delivery Plans, Scottish Water's Transformation Plan, performance reporting, and customer engagement. However, the periodic assessments showed that stakeholders continued to grapple with some aspects of SRC21 throughout the process, such as the openness of proceedings and the balance between collaboration and ownership.

- The EBRSG review that occurred **during the early months of the COVID-19 pandemic** showed new concerns related to the economic environment. Participants noted that COVID-19 and related developments placing political pressure on the outcome of SRC21. In addition, participants expressed some concerns about changing ways of working as the pandemic required a shift to remote working.

Box 3.3. EBR in the non-household market

WICS also regulates the retail non-household market, which has grown to include 29 retailers in 2020 (Citizens Advice Scotland, 2021, p. 4[9]). In response to the COVID-19 pandemic, the regulator introduced a range of measures to help the retail market weather shocks (WICS, 2020[10]). In 2021, the regulator created a working group for these "licensed providers" to consider proposals for measures that would help ensure the recovery and resilience of retailers in the wake of the COVID-19 crisis (WICS, 2021, p. 2[11]).

The group also presented the opportunity to experiment with a different approach in the retail non-household market. Inspired by ethical business regulation, the regulator encouraged retailers to take a collaborative approach in the working group to think collectively to improve the market framework. Participation in the working group was voluntary. CAS chaired the group, allowing guidance of the group to originate from an independent source. Indeed, WICS maintained frequent engagement with the group, but limited its formal involvement in an attempt to encourage the group to own its decisions. This represented a novel attempt to apply an EBR-inspired approach to a working group involving competitors in the sector.

The early impacts of the working group are appearing in changes in the regulatory approach for the retail non-household market, which provides advantages for licensed providers acting within what WICS considers to be good ethical business practice. Traditionally, WICS would have been prescriptive about new and changed license measures for retailers. In light of consultation and engagement with the working group and stakeholders, WICS decided to introduce voluntary license conditions in certain areas. In particular, licensed providers are welcomed to include license conditions in the areas of 1) a

---

new deferral scheme to support customers affected by COVID-19 and 2) a demonstration of financial resilience to WICS and Scottish Water. In its consultation response, WICS writes that such an approach is "consistent with encouraging licensed providers to take ownership for improving the market framework" (WICS, 2021, p. 6[11]). If licensed providers adopt either the financial resilience condition only or both of the conditions, they receive certain specified benefits, such as the relaxation of wholesale payment terms and limitations on customer pre-payments. In addition, licensed providers that do not include either condition are marked as "high risk providers" on the WICS website as they will not have participated in the "Market Health Check" of licensed providers' financial strength (WICS, 2021, p. 5[12]).

The constitution of the working group and the voluntary license conditions mark an early foray into applying ethical principles to the retail non-household market. The group encouraged ownership and collective thinking. In turn, the regulator defined clear advantages for behaviour in line with principles and clear consequences for behaviour that strays from principles.

Source: WICS, 2021.

WICS re-imagines the use of its powers to further EBR

WICS hopes that an EBR-inspired approach will ultimately produce benefits for the sector and the consumer, but it maintains its powers of discipline on standby. If the regulated company does not meet expectations, the regulator envisions a series of stages of escalatory actions on the part of the regulator. These actions will start small, such as seeking additional information from the company. The regulator plans to escalate proportionally to the severity of the company's action, with the most severe response being enforcement action. A key new skill for the regulator will be its ability to move up and down these escalatory steps. The regulator has summed this up in the "T" Diagram, pictured in Figure 3.2.

Figure 3.2. WICS's 'T' Diagram shows how it intends to escalate regulatory responses if necessary

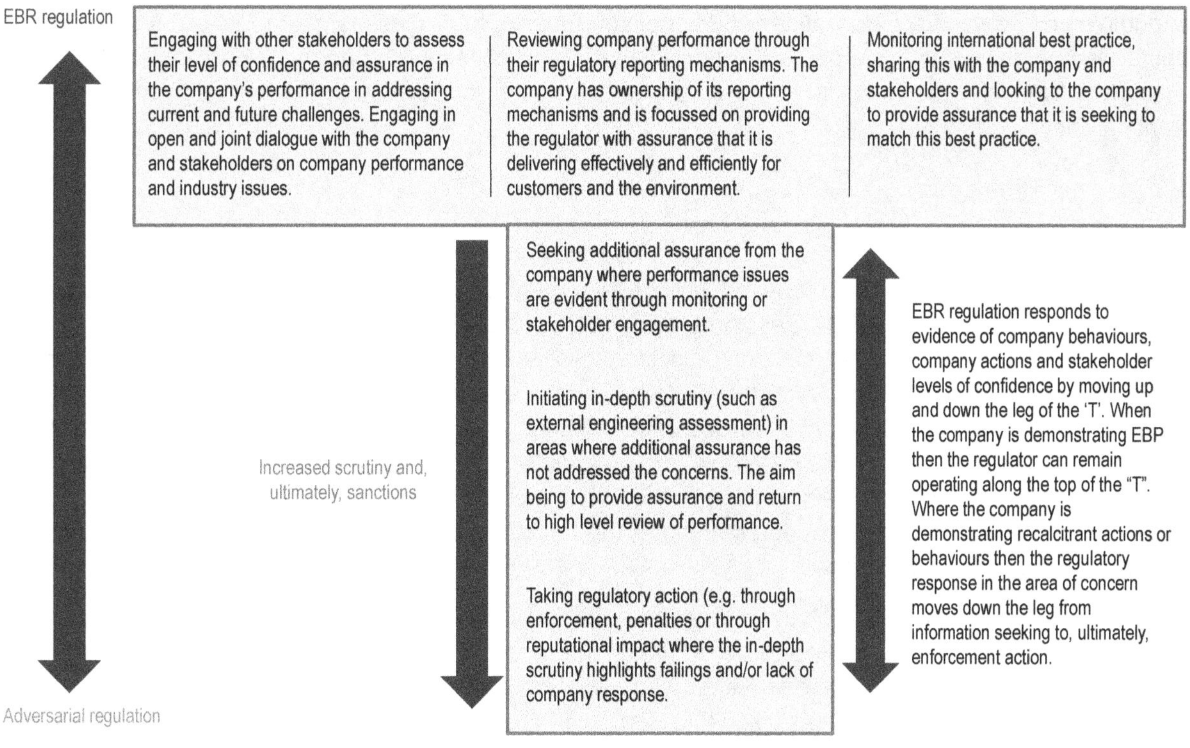

Source: WICS, 2021.

Looking forward: the challenges of moving away from the adversarial approach

Steps taken to change the relationship between the regulator and the regulated company, involving the other stakeholders as integral participants in the SRC21 process, presented value-added in the Scottish context in terms of increased trust. An EBR-inspired approach has produced valuable outcomes during and in the immediate aftermath of SRC21. Parties appreciated a new emphasis on learning during SRC21, which allowed all parties to advance towards final outputs together. Parties agree that the EBRSG was a useful outlet, allowing SRC21 participants to express sentiments and concerns that were reflected back to the group in an anonymous and constructive way. WICS and Scottish Water have adjusted their ways of working towards a more open exchange of information, and early reports suggest that participants feel the shift facilitates a more productive dialogue. WICS reports a reduction in around 20% in consultancy costs during this price review as compared to those previous, suggesting that changes in resource allocation accompanied new ways of working.

Introducing EBR and EBP principles into SRC21 has proved a challenging task as it requires new norms, culture and behavioural change, and new instruments. As the approach was relatively new and untested in its practical implementation, it faced roadblocks and required adjustments. Parties had to establish shared expectations, ensure that culture change permeated organisations, and translate loose principles into instruments. The innovative nature of SRC21 have made these challenges almost inevitable. Lessons from this experience should be taken into consideration for the preparation of the next SRC.

Investing in relationships and knowledge-building

The SRC21 process was demanding for participants, but created knowledge- and relationship-building advantages. Monthly stakeholder meetings, spin-off working group meetings, and "deep dive" sessions about aspects of Scottish Water's operations required considerable time investment from participants. Representatives were often from the highest levels of their organisations: the Stakeholder Advisory Group meetings brought together executive and senior representatives from each participant organisation. Opportunity costs for participant organisations, especially in light of intense and ongoing engagement with executive and senior staff, may justify additional streamlining of processes going forward. While the time costs were high, some stakeholders reported that the process was "worth it" due to the immediate outcomes from SRC21, including a "no surprises" approach for some outputs with a greater degree of transparency.

Establishing buy-in and expectations

An EBR- and EBP-inspired approach was a marked departure from what had been "business as usual" in the Scottish water sector, and required the development of buy-in and shared expectations among stakeholders. The methodology designed by WICS in 2017 at the outset of the SRC21 clarified expectations and inevitably left some of the practicalities of how to translate these expectations and EBR/EBP principles undefined. With the SRC21 process entering uncharted territory at full speed, the group had to start with a sketch of what EBR/EBP principles would look like in practice instead of a developed picture. While this was inevitable and potentially necessary, the lack of certainty created some discomfort among some stakeholders on "how to" move forward. WICS reports that identifying, communicating and developing understanding of the benefits of the new approach was a key method to moving forward despite uncertainty.

The revision of WICS's methodology in November 2018 clarified some of the practical next steps. These clarifications were a welcome step to allow stakeholders to take ownership of the process, while at the same time providing guidance and ideas on what ownership would mean in practice. In particular, WICS formalised the move from a business plan to a Strategic Plan, giving more clarity to Scottish Water on what to do and where to put resources.

Even as additional guidance clarified expectations in some areas, the lack of shared definition of co-creation for the Strategic Plan have caused uncertainty. The mechanism of co-creation promised to build trust and ensure that all stakeholders were all going in the same direction, but the process of co-creation was unclear at the start. In the absence of a shared definition for co-creation, expectations for the process ranged from elevated participation to collective drafting. Ultimately, co-creation of the Strategic Plan gave way to joint review to avoid compromising the need for Scottish Water to take ownership of its strategy.

In some ways, the EBR-inspired approach to SRC21 fell short of the early vision of EBR expressed in the guiding principles for co-creation. For example, the hallmark of the EBRSG was the anonymity that it provided to participants. While participants agreed that the EBRSG's feedback was constructive, the tool has not served to further an open exchange between parties on its own. The implementation period following SRC21 brings its own challenges. As the Strategic Plan becomes a living document that should steer the long-term direction of the regulated company, these uncertainties related to co-creation should be less of an issue. However, it will be important to define roles and expectations of the different stakeholders in inputting into the Plan's updates and revisions.

Clarifying roles and ownership

During SRC21, there was some ambiguity about the role of the regulator's decision papers and analysis: was the regulator setting broad boundaries or releasing conclusive and terminal analysis? From the beginning of SRC21, WICS intended to increase the ownership of Scottish Water over its decision making, with the desired is that Scottish Water no longer simply responds to regulator directives. As during the previous SRC, when WICS published a series of "issues papers," the regulator continued to publish regular papers to communicate its evolving understanding and expectations for the regulatory process. However, this time WICS chose to call these papers "*decision* papers," which suggested finality. The terminology communicated that the regulator was making decisions rather than participating in a process designed to promote the ownership that they were seeking. This perception created an unintended dynamic during the final stages of the SRC21 process, when the Customer Forum began its negotiations with Scottish Water. WICS established clear ranges for prices within a decision paper, and the Customer Forum turned to WICS to resolve key issues within these parameters instead of Scottish Water.

Fostering a culture change within each organisation

Stakeholders invested considerably into incorporating EBR-inspired principles into the SRC21 process itself, but successful implementation requires culture change and continuous adaptation and flexibility within the organisations. This culture change requires significant and ongoing effort from Scottish Water as it attempts to embody EBP, and from WICS as it meets the company's efforts with an adjusted EBR-inspired approach to its regulation. WICS expressed its high expectations for EBP in its Prospects for Prices decision paper:

> *Implementing pure EBP is not straightforward – it requires a company to go well beyond operating in an 'ethical' way. It involves businesses continually demonstrating evidence of their commitment to open, fair and candid behaviours that builds and maintains the trust of its stakeholders. This is a very high bar – but one which, as a public corporation, Scottish Water must achieve (WICS, 2020, p. 11[4]).*

Scottish Water and WICS have taken deliberate steps to facilitate the necessary change, starting with bilateral EBR sessions between Scottish Water and WICS. Each organisation is carrying on culture change work internally, as well. In co-operation with Ruth Steinholtz, an EBR and EBP pioneer in the academic world, WICS launched its work with a workshop on cultural values with its staff in September 2020. The Chief Operating Officer of WICS and Steinholtz have also engaged in EBR conversations with Scottish Water. This conversation broadened to include other stakeholders, with Steinholtz offering a webinar on EBP for all stakeholders.

Scottish Water's culture change challenge is interwoven with its transformation plan, which requires a shift in organisational culture and behaviours. Scottish Water began this process by engaging with its staff in "Scottish Water Character" conversations to identify aspects of company character that are consistent with future needs and expectations and those that should be shifted or developed. Scottish Water will integrate Scottish Water Character into the workings of the company by adding new modules and topics to a new leadership programme. Scottish Water contracted a management consultancy to take forward transformation planning activities within the company. An EBR and EBP expert will provide support during this process, with Ruth Steinholtz providing tailored input on relevant parts of the transformation planning exercise. Scottish Water has reported on its transformation planning regularly to the Stakeholder Advisory Group.

WICS has reflected information on shifts in its own organisation in its corporate plan. The regulator acknowledges that "the move to EBR will entail a transformation of our own," and describes how it is adjusting its corporate strategy and ways of working (WICS, 2021[13]). WICS identifies six key areas for development. Three of these areas target human resources, including recruitment, retention and development. The other three areas relate to the organisation's alignment with EBR/EBP, its agility and its transparency:

- "Developing understanding and capability" within WICS to implement the new behaviours and methods necessary for an EBR/EBP approach;
- "Increasing the flexibility, knowledge and communication" within WICS, including through functional integration;
- Enhancing WICS's capacity to carry out successful external communications, maintaining a conversation with stakeholders and improving communications to a broader audience (WICS, 2021, p. 27[13]).

Separately but in parallel, SEPA has been working with Chris Hodges to facilitate an EBR approach within the organisation. This work is in line with its regulatory strategy, One Planet Prosperity, which outlines a new approach to SEPA's enforcement strategy and states SEPA's support for businesses that want to go "beyond compliance" (SEPA, 2016[14]).

Translating principles into instruments

One of the key principles guiding SRC21 was "trust but verify," which WICS hoped would take the place of the parent-child relationship that had marked previous regulatory periods (WICS, 2017[15]). WICS was acutely aware from the beginning of SRC21 that the new trust environment should be accompanied by a verification mechanism that would further reinforce the mutual trust among the regulated company and the regulators. Defining how this principle would work in practice is a central question of SRC21 that will need to be addressed.

Early efforts to define this instrument came from the Reporting Performance and Information working group, which focused on the metrics of performance reporting. A "trust and confidence model" developed by WICS (discussed further in The performance reporting framework promises to maintain trust and confidence) aims to create a framework within which Scottish Water provides ample assurance that is delivering on its commitments in its Strategic Plan. The model shows the early contours of a performance framework that focuses on behavioural elements to complement formal measures of performance, aiming to create an EBR environment that favours openness and transparency. This approach seeks to assess the extent to which Scottish Water will effectively change organisational culture and behaviours. However, while the trust and confidence model offers some indication of how EBR and EBP principles will feature in the performance framework, parties do not have a collective expression of views on how principles will be translated into specific practice going forward.

Challenges associated with long-life assets and time-inconsistency of investment need

The starting point: A need for investment decisions to meet long-term challenges

Decisions on asset management today can affect consumers decades into the future, making a strategic approach to decision making about long-life assets critical. A number of stakeholders had expressed the view that the existing regulatory framework did not fully enable clear-eyed consideration of trade-offs between today's costs and future benefits. WICS felt the need to re-focus and clarify some of the approaches to SRC21. In its Methodology Refinements and Clarifications, WICS expressed that a focus on long-term maintenance, replacement and improvement of assets would become a precondition for the maintenance and improvement of service levels (WICS, 2018, p. 19[16]). Suboptimal investment for the long-term also has intergenerational equity implications, with current customers not paying the true costs for services.

While WICS's initial target was asset management, WICS and the stakeholder group began to consider climate change as another long-term challenge during the SRC. The need for aligning investment decisions with a long-term perspective became even more urgent as the SRC21 integrated an increasingly important focus on climate change. The "beyond net-zero" target set by the Scottish Government for Scottish Water created an urgent driver for the company to incorporate sustainability concerns into the core of its activities and to make investment decisions transparently. This includes understanding and communicating how investment decisions influence outcomes such as emissions reductions (WICS, 2017, p. 22[3]).

Faced with an asset replacement challenge and a net zero challenge, both involving significant uncertainty, the regulator saw a long-term perspective as a potential solution. The key question for SRC21 was how the regulatory framework would appropriately enable a long-term view. A long-term perspective would not be possible without a clear picture of needs and opportunities, which requires an understanding of asset conditions and high-quality appraisals that reflect strategic vision.

The regulator understood that a long-term perspective must be supported by strong financial discipline. The uncertainty around when increased funding will be necessary adds a significant complication to the regulatory framework. Infrastructure investment needs are notoriously "lumpy," requiring significant expenditure for a discrete and lasting investment, which may deliver the greater part of its usefulness to future generations. Balancing inflows and outflows of money when optimal expenditure is not constant and predictable becomes a greater challenge with a long-term approach.

The following sections present the approach in SRC21 to address the challenges of long-life assets and time-inconsistency of investment need. The first section describes efforts to improve the company's and stakeholders' awareness of capital needs in the short-, medium- and long-term through a Capital Maintenance Advisory Group. The second outlines the use of an asset management improvement plan and roadmap to chart the route forward. The third presents WICS's proposal for a longer regulatory period to better enable long-term planning and a response to COVID-19. The final section presents a new output for SRC21, a Strategic Plan from Scottish Water designed to promote strategic, long-term thinking.

Moving ahead: Squaring future needs with today's prices and investment

The Capital Maintenance Advisory Group helps the company and SRC21 parties understand investment needs

A precondition for a strategic long-term perspective to asset management was a robust understanding of the state of Scottish Water's assets and its needs for the future. In order to better understand the actual needs for an appropriate capital programme both for SRC21 and further into the future, WICS gathered a small group of experts (the Capital Maintenance Advisory Group) with experience in the regulated industries sector. The group met five times between 2017 and 2018; Scottish Water attended all meetings and produced an increasing amount of evidence with respect to the assets that are managed by the company and, consequently, the capital needs foreseen for the short, medium and long run.

The Group published its recommendations in April 2018. The recommendations identify the need for Scottish Water to strengthen and invest in its capacity to monitor and evaluate asset conditions and risks and develop an organisational culture that supports engagement with customers and communities around the asset stock. Those were endorsed by WICS and shared with SRC stakeholders.

The work of WICS and the Advisory Group on capital maintenance showed that long-term investment requirements were not well understood and pointed to unknowns and data gaps, and Scottish Water would have to dedicate significant effort to evidence its needs. For this, WICS proposed the creation of a comprehensive work plan defining actions and milestones. The performance monitoring regime would help Scottish Water share and evidence its progress. In addition, WICS made clear that the ring-fenced portion of Scottish Water's allowed revenues would be available when the company shows sufficient and verified progress against the work plan (WICS, 2018[17]).

An asset management improvement plan and roadmap chart the path forward

The conclusions of the Capital Maintenance Advisory Group made clear that the company would have to put in place appropriate planning to improve its asset management, from data to delivery. The asset management improvement plan and the asset management transformation roadmap offered the promise of improving data and building confidence that Scottish Water can deliver higher investment in a strategic way. The asset management improvement work benefited from ongoing external expertise and stakeholder scrutiny.

Working with an expert in infrastructure management, Scottish Water prepared a 10-year asset management improvement plan to improve information and decision making on assets. The process of developing the plan included a maturity assessment, with benchmarking of maturity scores against those of other companies in the water sector and other sectors. Asset management planning resulted in an asset management transformation roadmap that outlines the areas Scottish Water has identified for improvement and defines milestones and deliverables. This roadmap would be updated in an iterative process featuring input from stakeholders in an Asset Management Improvement working group, and an external expert will check progress against objectives in the improvement plan every year (Scottish Water, 2020[18]).

Consideration is given to long-term planning within a six-year regulatory period

From the discussions in the Advisory Group and initial brainstorming it also became increasingly clear that the six-year regulatory period was not providing the right incentives to think long-term and plan maintenance and investment in this perspective. While regulatory periods do not in principle prevent consideration for longer-term issues, they could provide an incentive to focus on the set regulatory horizon. An option to address this challenge would be to extend the regulatory periods.

The idea of progressively extending the regulatory periods took more and more prominence as the climate change challenges and net-zero target became an important focus of the discussions with parties. Ministers' principles of charging define a six-year period, but ministers considered proposals from WICS to adjust the length of the regulatory period to better respond to long-term challenges.

The COVID-19 crisis accelerated some of these discussions and provided an opportunity to anticipate and accelerate the thinking around a long-term perspective. In response to a request from the Cabinet Secretary for Environment, Climate Change and Land Reform, WICS laid out options to address the impact of COVID-19 on SRC21 in April 2020. In a letter to the Cabinet Secretary, WICS's Chief Executive underlined the importance of a response that makes sense for long-term asset replacement and climate challenges. According to WICS, a longer regulatory period would provide the Scottish Government with flexibility to manage the economic impacts of COVID-19 related to the water sector while maintaining sight of long-term strategic challenges.

WICS outlined several options for the start and length of the regulatory period to follow SRC21. Several options relate to the timing of the SRC21, the timing of the release of the final determination, and the end of the current regulatory period without significantly altering the regulatory period. Two options proposed a longer regulatory period, of either 12 or 15 years. WICS made a recommendation for such an extension, without voicing a preference for a 12- or 15-year extension.

An extension would have a range of implications, which WICS laid out in the same letter. Extending the regulatory period would require revisions of the government documents that launch and establish expectations for the SRC. WICS stated that an extended regulatory period would not necessarily require a long-term price profile or policy mix that would bind future administrations. To avoid this, it offered the mechanism of an average annual charge cap and charge floor over the full length of the regulatory period. Ministers could exercise flexibility within the longer period, providing input on how strategic objectives should be operationalised to the IPPG. WICS's modelling suggested that making use of flexibility would likely not change the long-term average annual cap and floor, short of a major change like a decision to advance or delay the net-zero target. In WICS's view, the fifteen-year period has some advantages over the twelve-year period. In addition to adding additional flexibility for charge profiles and available resources, the extra three years would allow WICS's to take into account final progress against Scottish Water's Asset Management Improvement Plan, even if delays result from the COVID-19 crisis (WICS, 2020[19]).

After considering the options, Ministers confirmed that the length of the regulatory period would remain the same in their final principles of charging in December 2020. However, the principles of charging underlined Ministers' support for long-term planning. They asked that "work be undertaken to prepare for the period beyond 31 March 2027," taking into account long-term challenges as well as evolving social and economic conditions (Scottish Government, 2020[20]).

Scottish Water's Strategic Plan is designed to enable a strategic approach to long-term challenges

Scottish Water's a Strategic Plan differs significantly from the Business Plans produced in previous price reviews. Previous Strategic Reviews of Charges would have produced a detailed Business Plan with a list of investment outputs and Scottish Water's view of price caps and borrowing needed to fund these projects. SRC21 resulted in a new type of document, one with fewer specifics but a greater emphasis on strategic vision. The enhanced role of stakeholders in the process, described in Stakeholders experiment with co-creation for Scottish Water's Strategic Plan, provided an ongoing challenge to Scottish Water, which ensured that themes important to stakeholders appeared in the final Strategic Plan.

An amended version of WICS's methodology, which the regulator published in November 2018, formalised a transition from the Business Plan to a Strategic Plan. The regulator also outlined key questions it expected Scottish Water to answer with its Strategic Plan (Box 3.4).

Box 3.4. WICS's expectations for Scottish Water's Strategic Plan

The WICS's revised regulatory methodology (November 2018) outlined some of the key questions that the regulator expected Scottish Water to consider in co-creating its Strategic Plan with stakeholders.

- What are the expectations that customers and communities have for the water industry that will serve their children and grandchildren?

> - How does Scottish Water propose to meet and exceed these expectations in doing the right thing for customers, communities, stakeholders and Scotland more generally?
> - How will Scottish Water meet the compliance requirements of its quality regulators?
> - How will it address the challenges identified in its Strategic Projections? Which of these challenges need urgent attention?
> - How long does Scottish Water believe it can reasonably take to transition to the point where it is fully funded to meet these obligations?
> - How does Scottish Water believe its prices will need to change to accommodate this expenditure?
> - How does Scottish Water propose to build the confidence of its customers, communities and other stakeholders in its management of this transition?
> - How will Scottish Water develop as an organisation in the light of the Commission's revised approach to economic regulation?
> - What does Scottish Water believe that it will need from its stakeholders?
>
> Source: WICS (2018), "Strategic Review of Charges 2021-27: Methodology refinements and clarifications", https://wics.scot/publications/price-setting/strategic-review-charges-2021-27/approach/2021-27-methodology-refinements.

The process of drafting a Strategic Plan started with Strategic Projections developed by Scottish Water, which were subject to formal consultation and scrutiny by the Customer Forum. These Projections would identify long-term challenges and develop a transparent strategy to address those and improve performance, with the goal of feeding into the Strategic Plan. Scottish Water published a draft Strategic Projections document in February 2018, with a consultation period running through August (Scottish Water, 2018[21]). In addition to the formal consultation, Scottish Water discussed earlier drafts of the document with the Customer Forum in two high-level meetings attended by the CEO and senior management of Scottish Water. These provided an opportunity for the Forum to challenge Scottish Water on the knowledge of their asset base, the assumptions used to derive future trends and their ability to reflect lessons from the customer experience indices into forward planning.

WICS and stakeholders provided their reactions during the comment period, pushing Scottish Water to increase the ambition of the projections. WICS reacted to the document in its first Decision Paper July 2018 that contributed also to enriching the evidence provided by Scottish Water (see Annex A for a summary of the regulator's decision papers). SEPA, DWQR, and CAS also submitted responses to Scottish Water's Strategic Projections in August 2018. In line with the Customer Forum's reaction, regulators and consumer bodies outlined a range of opportunities for improving the scope and content of the Strategic Projections, with one overarching theme: the need to plan for long-term challenges in a more ambitious, strategic, measurable and inclusive way.

Scottish Water had another opportunity to rise to meet stakeholder expectations in its Strategic Plan. Scottish Water published a detailed outcome report with the results of the consultation on the Strategic Projections and its planned responses. However, WICS confirmed with Scottish Water that the Strategic Plan would supersede the Strategic Projections, allowing Scottish Water to focus on producing a Strategic Plan reflecting the views of stakeholders rather than honing final Strategic Projections.

Building on the Strategic Projections, Scottish Water presented its first Outline Strategic Plan in December 2018. At the core of the Plan were four key ambitions: to support a flourishing Scotland; to deliver a consistently leading customer experience; to improve the reliability, resilience and sustainability of service to customers; and to treat customers' money with respect. Each ambition was underpinned by 3-4 strategic outcomes, which in turn were supported by a series of activities.

Through an informal consultation, stakeholders sent the message to Scottish Water to strengthen the strategic approach and vision underlying the outline Strategic Plan Scottish Water collected written feedback from all stakeholders on the Outline Strategic Plan in spring 2019. The main criticisms received were that the vision ("Trusted to care for the water on which Scotland depends") was not strong enough - and that the Plan was too focused on operational matters and less on strategic priorities. Scottish Water responded to the feedback received in a dedicated session of the SAG.

Work on the Strategic Plan continued with bi- and multi-lateral meetings between Scottish Water and SRC stakeholders. In June 2019, stakeholders gathered for a two-day discussion on key milestones of SRC21. They discussed the elements of Scottish Water's draft Strategic Plan, contributing to finalising the strategic outcomes. The development of the shared sector vision helped streamline the overarching objectives. The intervening changes in climate policies also set emissions reductions and renewable energy at the forefront of the Plan. A September 2019 draft was more ambitious and less heavy on details, reflecting stakeholder comments.

In January 2020, Scottish Water and the Customer Forum entered into a "Minute of Agreement on the Strategic Plan." The document states "[t]he Customer Forum considers the Strategic Plan has taken proper account of the evidence provided on the views and aspirations of current and future customers." It notes areas of the Strategic Plan where the Customer Forum sought further assurance, and details how Scottish Water addressed or will address their concerns (Scottish Water and Customer Forum, 2020[22]). The Minute of Agreement was followed by the publication of the final Strategic Plan in February 2020. The final Strategic Plan reflects considerable progress as a result of the collaborative process.

Scottish Water's final Strategic Plan outlines the company's central strategic outcomes, driven by the overall purpose of supporting a flourishing Scotland. It defines three overarching outcomes: beyond net zero emissions; great value and financial sustainability; and service excellence (Figure 3.3). Each objective is underpinned by several strategic objectives, which outline how the company will achieve the strategic objectives. Through a collaborative process, Scottish Water's Strategic Plan came to feature many of the themes important to stakeholders, notably the focus on climate adaptation and mitigation (advocated by the Forum, SEPA and DWQR) and the importance of empowering customers and communities.

WICS acknowledged the progress represented by the Strategic Plan in its draft determination, while recognising its limitations (WICS, 2020[23]). According to WICS, the Strategic Plan was guided by a clear vision and bolstered by an extensive research programme. It reflects the "no surprises" approach pursued in SRC21, while still serving as an important initial step towards Scottish Water taking ownership over its strategy. However, WICS argues that the Strategic Plan also represents "something of a missed opportunity," saying that the company could have made implications on charges and plans to mitigate impacts on charges more explicit (WICS, 2020, p. 5[23]).

Figure 3.3. Scottish Water's Strategic Plan

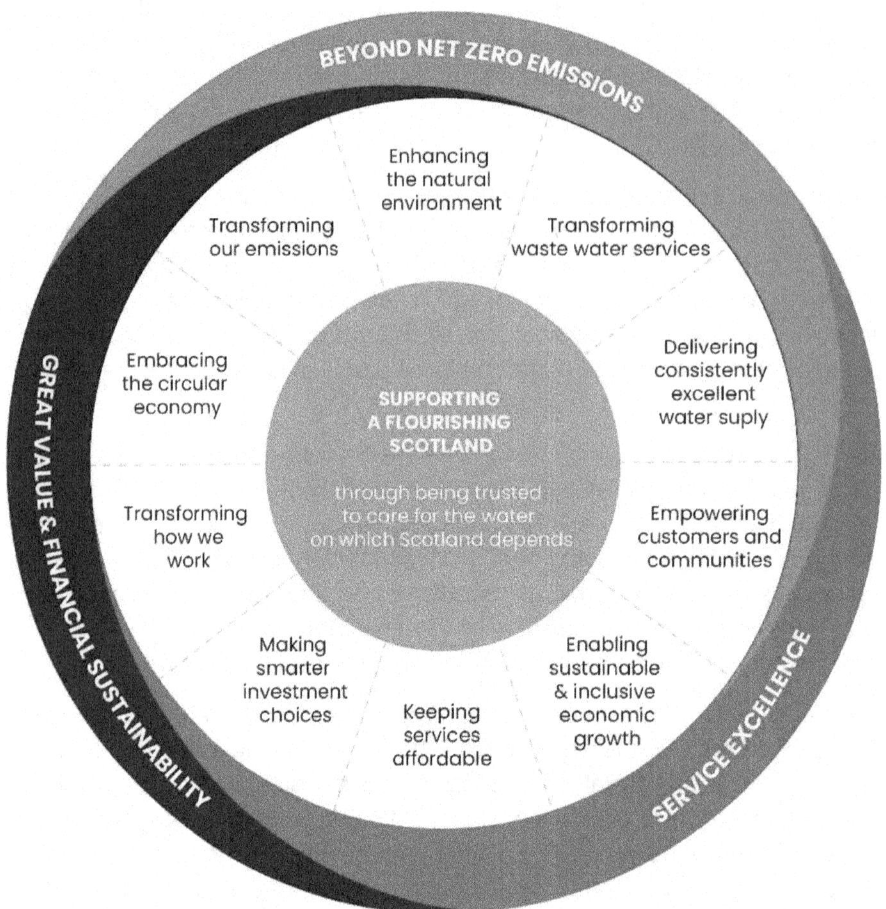

Source: Scottish Water (2020), "A Sustainable Future Together", https://www.scottishwater.co.uk/help-and-resources/document-hub/key-publications/strategic-plan.

A net zero roadmap sketches planned movement towards an ambitious goal

Scottish Water, a major user of electricity in Scotland, agreed to meet a net zero objective set in the Scottish Government's 2019 Programme for Scotland. Scottish Water is the largest purchaser of electricity and the fastest growing sector in Scotland, although it also produces a significant amount of renewable energy relative to its usage. As an energy intensive industry marked by the presence of a large, state-owned service provider, the water sector was a natural target for government climate action. The Scottish Government announced in its 2019 Programme for Scotland that Scottish Water would commit to becoming "zero carbon user of electricity by 2040", five years before the national net zero target in 2045 (Scottish Government, 2019, p. 53[24]). The government programme provides the broad contours of an ambitious shift for Scottish Water, including a commitment to produce or host three times of the electricity it uses with renewable energy.

Scottish Water responded to this challenge by charting a course towards net zero operational and embodied carbon. In response to the government programme, Scottish Water developed a net zero roadmap in consultation with an expert panel and stakeholders to guide actions towards the net zero goal. The roadmap explains that the company will go beyond conventional carbon accounting to take into account all emissions associated with the company's activities, including both operational and embodied carbon and looking to the supply chain. Investment emissions along the supply chain are new challenge for Scottish Water and thus a focus of the roadmap; Scottish Water reports that it is developing a measure of carbon intensity of investment to understand and address emissions from these sources.

The roadmap attempts to guide the steps towards decarbonising the company's activities while maintaining service levels, establishing two intermediate goals before the 2040 objective. In 2025, Scottish Water plans to reduce operational emissions by at least 60% and advance in its understanding of investment emissions enough to set a new goal in this area for 2030. In 2030, the goal for reductions in operational emissions increases to at least 75%. It outlines the improvements the company would like to make in specific areas – electricity, process emissions, gas and fuel oil use, transport and travel, investment, and carbon storage – with some intermediate goals defined. The intermediate goals tend to be qualitative (for example, one 2040 goal is "[a]ll projects routinely demonstrate they have minimised emissions as far as possible"). Scottish Water plans to review progress against the roadmap and make necessary updates annually in consultation with stakeholders (Scottish Water, n.d.[25]).

Looking forward: taking a long-term view to regulating the water sector

Connecting the dots between asset management and strategic ambitions

Asset management planning is a key determinant of the successful delivery of Scottish Water's strategic ambitions. The Strategic Plan does not establish a plan to achieve its ambitions, which could be a challenge as it could weaken its applicability and impact. Planning products such as the asset management planning improvement plan and roadmap promise to establish the short-term, intermediate and long-term steps necessary to deliver the ambitions. This approach could help at least identify the need to plan ahead. However, the ambition, robustness and effectiveness of asset management planning and implementation must be commensurate with the challenge of delivering the Strategic Plan. WICS emphasises the importance of institutional transformation to deliver the Strategic Plan in its final determination, stating that "[t]his final determination is underpinned by the expectation that Scottish Water will undergo the fundamental transformation necessary to deliver its part in the long-term vision set out in its Strategic Plan" (WICS, 2020, p. 16[6]).

WICS, aware of the risk that the company's asset management approach could fall short of delivering on long-term objectives, asked Scottish Water to work with a strategy consultant to make necessary refinements. This would occur under the umbrella of transformation planning, discussed further in Clarifying roles and ownership.

The transformation plan under development by Scottish Water has an aim of transforming decision making and cultural practice from top to bottom. The company's transformation plan promises to provide critical direction on *how* the company will deliver and evolve. This includes the company's relationship with its customers whereby the commitment is to "take every decision as if the customer were in the room" (discussed further in Expanding beyond normal consultation). It will be crucial to see the extent to which the transformation plan identifies concrete milestones and indicators of the extent to which this transformation is embedded across the company, including indicators relating to customers and front-line services that are key in understanding needs and ensuring effective delivery.

Evidencing the needs for investment decisions

The Capital Maintenance Advisory Group has contributed to broadening the perspective and learning from other regulated industries. Lessons and evidence from other industries on how long-term risks are addressed have proved particularly relevant for understanding how the state of the assets and future needs are assessed and evaluated for. This approach appears to have proved useful not only for the regulated company but also for WICS and the other regulators involved in the process. The challenge is now to ensure that the data and evidence is continuously produced and, crucially, shared and used to take investment decisions and alert on new needs. As the SRC21 ends and WICS is planning ahead for the next SRC, there is the need to think of an evolution of the Advisory Group. The cross-industry sharing of experience and learning probably need to be complemented by even stronger inputs and advice on how to produce and use data and evidence.

Equally important is to ensure that the data is shared candidly and early. Acknowledging information asymmetries between the regulator and the regulated entity is one of the foundations of economic regulation. An EBR approach aims to develop a relationship between the regulator and company that is marked by trust and transparency, bringing with it the promise of reducing the information asymmetry. Scottish Water's candid sharing of data on its assets and the collaborative working between Scottish Water and WICS to develop the company's ability to deliver its strategic objectives are early wins for EBR within this context. Going forward, being open on any early indication of risks could become a key feature of the approach, taking also advantage of the Ethical Business Regulation concept that has informed the SRC21.

Addressing trade-offs

The strong focus on climate change and achieving net-zero emissions will pose a number of challenges for asset management and investment. There will be inevitable trade-offs between, for example, maintaining and investing in new assets, emission impacts and, possibly, community and customer focus. These trade-offs will need to be made explicit and addressed with the help of the regulators. Research conducted during the SRC21 showed that, when challenge of asset replacement and net zero were clear, customers were behind it. Research and engagement will need to continue to make sure as operational decisions are taken, the public is made aware of the choices made and the rationale behind them.

Taking a regulatory long-term view

The SRC21 approach has embedded a strong focus on taking a long-term view to regulating the water industry. Despite WICS's recommendation that a longer regulatory period would promote strategic long-term thinking, some stakeholders expressed doubts on the effectiveness of a longer period in ensuring that the regulated industry delivers and is held accountable. Ultimately, the extension of the SRC period was not enacted. However, the unfortunate circumstance of the COVID-19 pandemic fit into on-going thinking on the SRC's timeline and accelerated discussions with Ministers on the opportunity to lengthen the regulatory periods.

While stopping short of extending the regulatory period, ministers have nevertheless supported a long-term planning approach. How to "square the circle" then? While much of the discussion arising from SRC21 points to long-term planning, intermediate "checkpoints" will be critical to maintain confidence that the company continues to deliver in line with its commitments on all time-scales. The concerns expressed by some stakeholders point to the need to put in place safeguards and regular checks that leave space for adjustments and does not give the impression that the process is on a sort of autopilot. The six-year regulatory period provides a natural point of assessment, while other processes provide ongoing feedback about Scottish Water's delivery and performance. As the industry looks ahead to the regulatory period and the goals beyond the period, it will be important that the suite of checkpoints provide actionable information about Scottish Water's progress towards long-term goals to the right audiences.

Flexibility of investment

The starting point: A rigid framework discourages ownership and innovation

As WICS considered a shift towards a long-term perspective, it was clear that a regulatory framework that supported better decision making in the industry for the short-, medium- and long-term would also require a commensurate level of flexibility. In previous regulatory periods, Scottish Water and quality regulators would settle on a list of investment requirements to achieve Ministers' objectives and statutory obligations, and Scottish Water's business plan (vetted by WICS) would establish how the company planned to deliver. This approach had several secondary consequences:

- It discouraged company ownership over investment decisions. In providing the regulator an opportunity for scrutiny and challenge to the business plan, the framework shifted responsibility away from the company to the regulator.
- It restricted innovative thinking. The business plan gave Scottish Water one opportunity for innovation, and the company always defined a "plan B" to ensure that obligations were met. While a ring-fenced fund promised to fund innovative projects in the last regulatory period, it was underutilised.
- It incentivised decision making based on lowest monetary cost over the regulatory control period. A focus on pure monetary cost provided limited consideration of non-monetary evaluations of costs and benefits in the short- and long-term. Combined with a self-contained, fixed regulatory period, the framework did not incentivise long-term initiatives when the payback occurred beyond the control period (WICS, 2018, p. 48[16]). Instead, the company may opt for initiatives without the same long-term benefits but with a lower cash outlay (including "sweating" assets, finding ways to extract additional value out of existing assets), freeing up resources to build a buffer or spend on other priorities.

From the beginning of SRC21, WICS envisioned replacing the "list of projects" with a more flexible arrangement that would enable decision making based on highest value rather than lowest cost. WICS planned to lower the barrier to money entering the business, providing a level of funding consistent with attaining long-term goals. In parallel, the regulatory framework would raise the barrier to money exiting the business in terms of investment, increasing the company's obligation to evidence its investment and decision making.

The regulator planned to use several tools to create a more flexible framework: a flexible system to prioritise investment and a "ring fenced" allowances that would become available only in certain circumstances. These tools would be supported by improved investment appraisals from the company, allowing Scottish Water to demonstrate that it had selected the highest-value investment. Stakeholders agreed with the regulator that appraisals could be strengthened with the consideration of non-monetary benefits, like carbon, social capital, and natural capital. Unlike the previous regulatory framework, this approach promised to promote innovation and widen the scope of benefits considered in investment decision making, advancing progress towards long-term goals.

The sections that follow show the new mechanisms emerging from SRC21 designed to increase the flexibility of the system. The first section explores the Investment Planning and Prioritisation Framework, which enables a flexible rolling approach to investment decisions that mainstreams stakeholder input. The second section describes WICS's final determination, which created a ring-fenced fund accessible for investment expenditure that is higher-cost, but higher value on a whole-life basis. The third section presents early ideas of a performance reporting framework designed to maintain trust and confidence that the company is delivering upon its strategic objectives.

Moving ahead: providing a more flexible and accountable investment framework

A new governance framework allows for a flexible, rolling approach to investment decisions

The Investment Planning and Prioritisation Framework is an important output of the SRC process as a key enabler of a more flexible but accountable investment approach. The final result of stakeholder processes described below is a governance framework that allows for rolling investment decisions with enhanced stakeholder input, rather than a six-year fixed investment programme. While Scottish Water maintains the responsibility for making decisions on planning and prioritisation and retain responsibility for outcomes, the process allows for greater flexibility and input from stakeholders.

The flexible process promises to offer benefits in terms of process and outcome. In its 2018 Decision Paper 3, WICS defined how a more flexible investment planning and prioritisation process would benefit consumers, communities and the supply chain. Consumers and communities would benefit from better responsiveness to needs, the supply chain would benefit from longer-term visibility on investment, and all would benefit from Scottish Water's commitment to more long-term strategic projects. The paper outlined a vision for investment planning and prioritisation whereby Scottish Water involves stakeholders in recording an extensive list of investments and stakeholders would help with an initial prioritisation, Scottish Water would develop appraisals for priority investments, and Scottish Water would take into account further stakeholder input when deciding which projects make the final list (WICS, 2018[26]).

A short-term stakeholder working group developed the outlines of the new governance framework. The Investment Planning and Prioritisation Framework working group was charged with developing a framework to facilitate engagement and build trust in investment decision making. The working group set out the key steps involved in the IPPF (Figure 3.4). The IPPF is marked by its enhanced accountability, with several opportunities for stakeholder input and ministerial approval and a transparent document trail recording the results of the process over time.

Figure 3.4. From a "long list" to a "committed list" through the IPPF

Needs and opportunities are narrowed down progressively until a "committed list" is reached

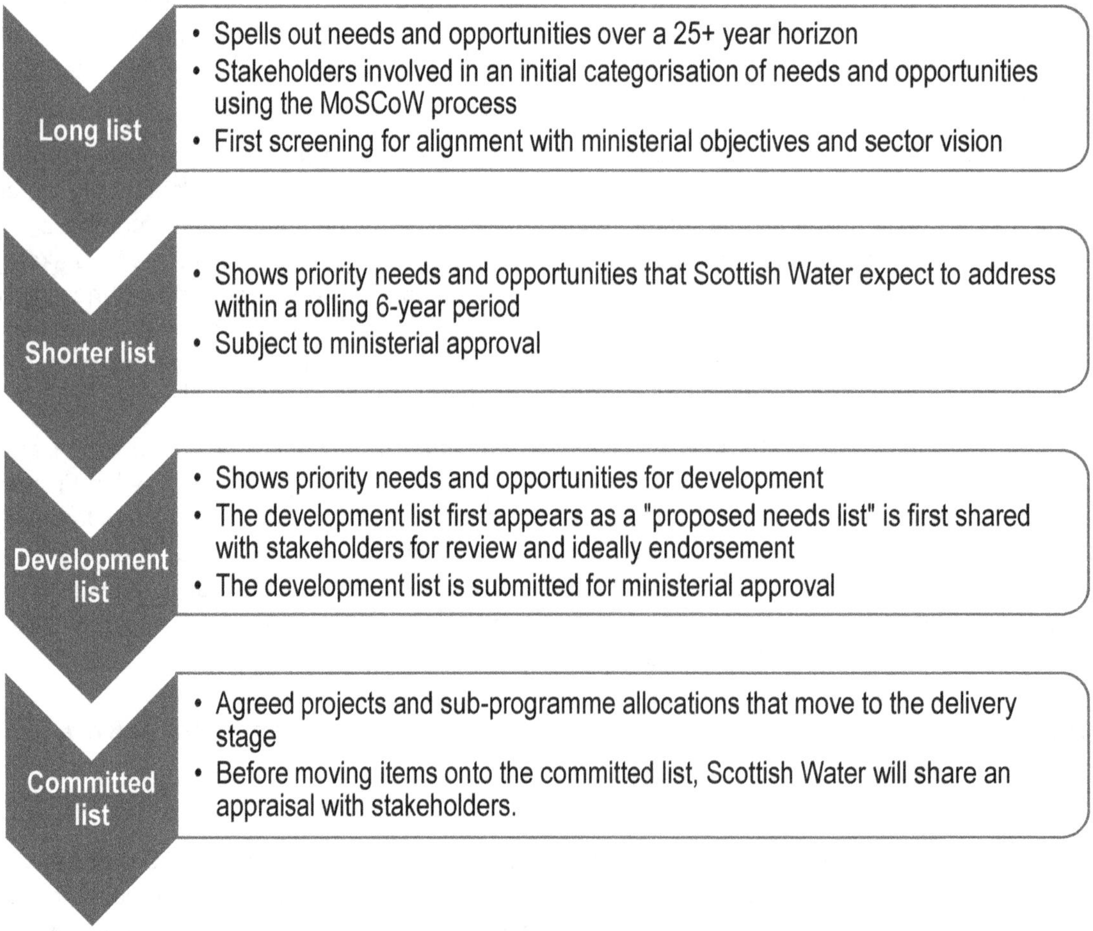

Long list
- Spells out needs and opportunities over a 25+ year horizon
- Stakeholders involved in an initial categorisation of needs and opportunities using the MoSCoW process
- First screening for alignment with ministerial objectives and sector vision

Shorter list
- Shows priority needs and opportunities that Scottish Water expect to address within a rolling 6-year period
- Subject to ministerial approval

Development list
- Shows priority needs and opportunities for development
- The development list first appears as a "proposed needs list" is first shared with stakeholders for review and ideally endorsement
- The development list is submitted for ministerial approval

Committed list
- Agreed projects and sub-programme allocations that move to the delivery stage
- Before moving items onto the committed list, Scottish Water will share an appraisal with stakeholders.

Source: Adapted from Scottish Water (2019), "Investment Planning and Prioritisation Framework: SR21 Strategic Plan Supporting Document," October 2019.

A second stakeholder working group established a preliminary approach to the prioritisation process. The IPPG WG developed a first approach to prioritising investment, which will be taken forward in the Investment Planning and Prioritisation Group (IPPG). This group is tasked with overseeing the development of Scottish Water's rolling investment programme and monitoring progress towards ministerial objectives, Scottish Water's Strategic plan and the sector vision.

The Scottish Government presented a draft ToR for the IPPG at the group's first meeting in August. The Government chairs the group, which brings together Scottish Water, WICS, the quality regulators, CAS and the Scottish Public Services Ombudsman.

The draft ToR outlines the responsibilities of the IPPG, which include:

- reviewing tranches of priority needs proposed by Scottish Water;
- reviewing progress towards the development of needs on the list;
- maintaining a mechanism enabling changes to the Strategic Investment Projections (data and information Scottish Water pulls together to inform their investment programme); and
- the short list of investment needs and opportunities. The draft ToR includes a foresight function for the IPPG, which includes reviewing the long-term vision and trajectories towards the vision and strategy, and considering whether they remain "relevant, achievable and fit for purpose".

The IPPG will also have reporting duties; the draft ToR states that the group will oversee the development of a monitoring framework for reporting actions and progress to ministers. The ToR is a live document and remains remain subject to review.

SRC21 maintains the Delivery Assurance Group (DAG), formed in 2006 as the Output Monitoring Group (OMG) to monitor the delivery of committed output. During the regulatory period following SRC21, the DAG will be supported by its own working group.

WICS's determination allows flexibility, incorporates natural and social capital

WICS draft determination, published in October 2020, submits the regulator's conclusions to public scrutiny and comment. The document fulfils its central purpose of sharing and justifying WICS's view of maximum charges over the forthcoming regulatory period. It also describes the inputs and process supporting the decision and reflects on next steps. The draft and final determinations formalise the shift from the regulator imposing a fixed price profile over time to the regulator allowing for flexibility in how Scottish Water uses charges.

The draft determination includes two main components related to charges:

- **A CPI+2% cost increase and an efficiency challenge:** Stressing there is no evidence that COVID-19 would affect the long-run assumptions WICS used in earlier estimates in the long term, WICS proposed an average CPI+2% cap on charges over the coming regulatory period. The CPI+2% cap is the annual average over the period, and Scottish Water will shape the trajectory of charges through annual Schemes of Charges proposing price levels for the coming year. WICS welcomes Scottish Water's suggestion to hold a "national conversation" while developing Scheme of Charges proposals.

   This increase is on the high end of the 1-2% range established in its earlier Prospects for Prices paper, which is consistent with WICS earlier messaging on this issue. It also establishes a 1% real efficiency challenge for Tier 1 expenditure (including operating costs, reactive maintenance, PFI costs, and interest) and a £150 million efficiency challenge for capital investment efficiency.

- **A ring-fenced allowance to account for including externalities in investment decisions:** WICS defined an annual allowance for investment in asset enhancement and growth of £300 million, an amount that does not include the £1,020 million of allowed borrowing from the Scottish

Government. The draft determination takes into account potential additional costs from considering externalities such as carbon emissions, natural capital and social capital in Scottish Water's investment decisions. WICS states that a special ring-fenced allowance of £133 million in 2017-18 prices (137 million updated for inflation) will be available to cover Scottish Water's costs when it selects options with a higher risk-adjusted Net Present Value. The IPPG will be responsible for approving requests to access the ring-fenced funds, after Scottish Water evidences need with appraisals.

The draft determination ends by emphasising the need for industry transformation and significant progress on emissions reductions to deliver the Ministerial Objectives. It includes the requirement for Scottish Water to produce a transformation plan that establishes a path for the company through the end of the regulatory period and to 2040, updated annually or bi-annually (WICS, 2020[23]).

The draft attracted 11 comments during the six-week comment period, including comments from Scottish Water, CAS, DWQR, SEPA, an environmental umbrella organisation, a tenants association, a local council, a trade organisation representing the supply chain, and three individuals (WICS, 2020[27]). The responses from bodies involved in the Stakeholder Advisory Group show alignment in thinking, but CAS and DWQR emphasise that the new regulatory framework should not negatively affect the issues under their purview – consumer welfare and drinking water quality (see Box 3.5 for a summary of these responses). Other responders emphasised issues such as costs, service quality, and supply chain preparedness.

Box 3.5. Formal responses from the Stakeholder Advisory Group to the draft determination

Reactions from **Scottish Water** on the draft determination reflect alignment after three years of collaborative working. Scottish Water's CEO welcomed the draft determination and stressed that further investment would be necessary to maintain service levels while addressing the twin challenges of climate change and aging infrastructure. He restates the company's commitment to undergoing the "radical transformation" to become a more open, transparent and iterative organisation (Millican, 2020[28]).

CAS's response acknowledges the necessity of price increases to protect service levels while investing in infrastructure, noting that principles of intergenerational equity require that current and future customers shoulder a "fair share" of long-term investment needs (CAS, 2020[29]). CAS's response also highlights considerations related to the impact of water charges on low-income households and in the context of economic recovery. It asserts that, even as average prices rise over the regulatory period, the percent of weekly income paid by low-income customers eligible for the Water Charges Reduction scheme should not increase. It suggests that Scottish Water consider limiting price increases in the first years of the regulatory period to "provide much needed breathing space recovering from the impact of COVID-19" (p. 1[29]).

DWQR's response emphasises the importance of maintaining service standards and investing in aging assets. It notes that drinking water quality is an area where England and Wales outperform Scotland, suggesting that this underlines the need for additional investment and improvement. It notes that a 99.92% compliance rate with standards has remained stable despite investment, and stresses that Scottish Water's compliance should not deteriorate further. The regulator welcomes the paradigm shift towards appraisals incorporating longer-term benefits, but emphasises that replacing aging assets that threaten to compromise quality standards should not be delayed. It also echoes concerns expressed throughout the process, that a more flexible system of investment decision making fails to provide certainty to quality regulators about the timescales for addressing needs (Millican, 2020[28]).

SEPA's comment emphasises the synergies between the proposal and relevant sector policy and strategy. It states that investment and transformation are necessary ingredients to delivering Scottish Government's Water Sector Vision and SEPA's One Planet Prosperity strategy. It strongly endorses the incorporation of natural and social capital in investment appraisals and expresses its willingness to work with the regulator and company to ensure that the ring-faced allowance delivers upon its promise (Ahearn, 2020[30]).

Source: WICS. (2020). Consultation Responses. Retrieved December 17, 2020, from https://www.watercommission.co.uk/view_Consultation_Responses.aspx.

The final determination, published in December 2020, echoes the main conclusions of the draft determination and adjusting slightly based on updated financial modelling. The final determination maintains the CPI+2% average cap on charges and the efficiency challenges. Several changes – the extension of a water charges reduction scheme, an updated inflation rate, an additional GBP 10 million for borrowing from the Scottish Government, and updated Scottish Water financial performance information – affected the financial modelling, but not enough to change this value. It adjusts the level of the ring-fenced allowance, lowering it slightly to GBP 132 million in 2017-18 prices (WICS, 2020[6]).

The final determination clarifies the ring-fenced allowance in response to comments received, emphasising alignment between the objective of the allowance and national environmental strategy. Indeed, SEPA and WICS sent a joint letter to Scottish Water explaining how the concept will enable decision making consistent with national environmental goals. The fund's objective to incorporate consideration of all relevant capitals, including social and natural, in appraisals and resulting investment decisions will further SEPA's One Planet Prosperity strategy (WICS, 2020[6]). In the letter, they stress that the allowance should not function as a cap on spending to support One Planet Prosperity (p. 19[6]).

The final determination marks a significant departure from thinking at the beginning of SRC21. Initially, parties hoped to ensure financial sustainability for Scottish Water, continuing to offer improvements in service while phasing out government borrowing. The conversation shifted over the course of SRC21, driven by multiple factors. As Scottish Water prepared its strategic projections and as more information on asset state came to light, it became clear that investment needs were much higher than expected. Furthermore, the net-zero goal introduced a new challenge. Taking these factors (among others) into account produced the ultimate parameters of the final determination: including the elements of an increase in the charge cap, specified levels of borrowing, an efficiency challenge, and the ring-fenced fund.

The performance reporting framework promises to maintain trust and confidence

During EBR Support Group assessments, some stakeholders expressed a desire for performance reporting to go beyond metrics. The trust and confidence model, once finished, has the promise to offer reassurance to stakeholders in line with an EBR/EBP approach. The trust and confidence model would add a new level of engagement on top of existing mechanisms for assurance, such as Scottish Water's audit committee. WICS has been working with consultants to develop the model, starting with stakeholder engagement sessions in March 2020 to understand expectations for reassurance. The resulting draft model (reproduced in Figure 3.5) reflects elements stakeholders think are important to create an open and transparent environment going forward. Instead of defining processes, it illustrates necessary behaviours. Key to the model is Scottish Water's provision of adequate reassurance in three areas: (1) investment planning and delivery, (2) transformation plan development and delivery, and (3) performance and the company's culture of service delivery. Scottish Water's reassurance becomes a feedback loop, with the company disclosing information openly and transparently, and stakeholders actively engaging with Scottish Water.

Key to the success of the feedback loop are several behavioural elements, identified in the model:

- Communication takes place in an environment of openness and transparency,
- Mistakes and failures are treated as learning opportunities,
- Collective shared responsibility and mutual understanding.

Figure 3.5. Draft trust and confidence model

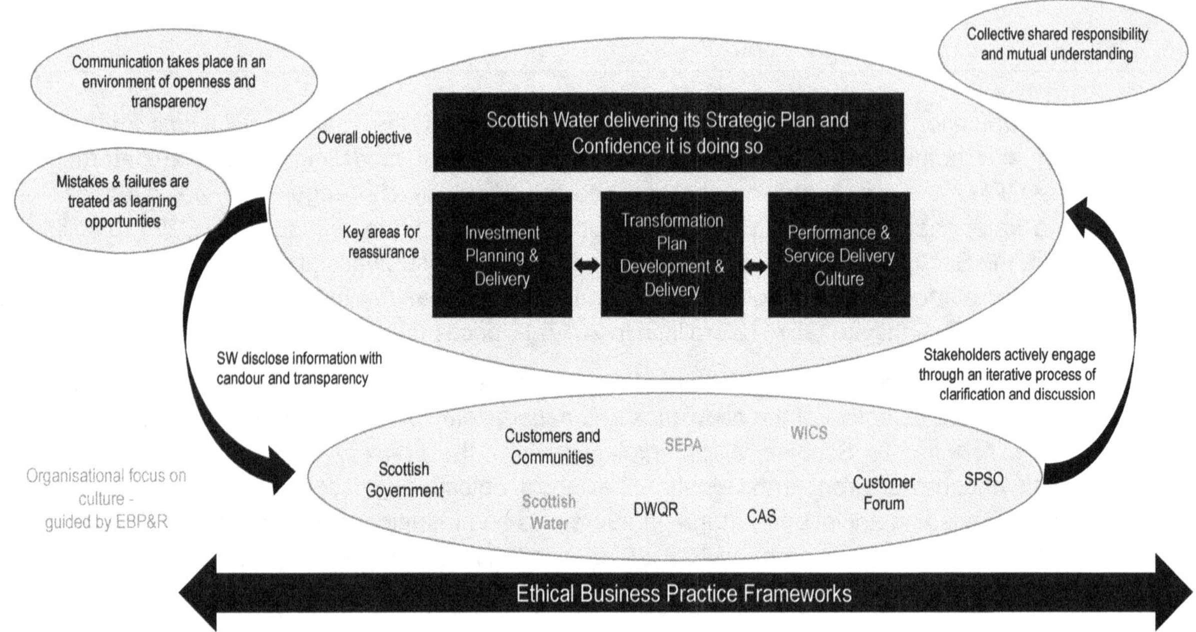

Source: WICS, Black & Veatch, Oakdene Advisory, Aretework (2020).

Looking forward: ensuring that the greater flexibility translates into innovation

The SRC21 has created space for addressing climate change challenges over the long-term through innovation and flexible investment. Looking ahead, the challenge will be to ensure that this opportunity is taken up and leads to continuous improvements. The previous SRC included already ring-fenced funds that could be used to support innovative projects, but the take up and impact of these ring-fenced funds are not evident. Ultimately, the impact of the added flexibility will depend on the capability of Scottish Water to appraise projects in a way that allows for innovation, as well as the willingness to take up risks and experiment.

Providing flexibility without compromising accountability

A system offering a previously unheard-of level of flexibility is underpinned by trust, and maintaining accountability will be key. Appropriate accountability will help Scottish Water provide confidence to Ministers that processes are functioning at an adequate level and that issues are being resolved. In addition, Scottish Water remains accountable to customers and communities, and must demonstrate that its decision making is in their best interest now and in the long term.

Performance assessment will be one tool to promote accountability, and the new system requires a new approach to performance reporting. A long-term perspective might imply that not all impacts will be evident and traceable within a single SRC. This calls for a monitoring framework that is continuous rather than cyclical. During the regulatory period that follows SRC21, the Scottish Government will maintain the Delivery Assurance Group, formed in 2006 as the Output Monitoring Group (OMG) to monitor the delivery of committed output. A key success factor of the group will be the choice of a set of indicators that allow for checking on continuous progress, with a mix of process indicators tracking how projects and investment needs are assessed and determined and intermediate outcome indicators that tracks progress towards long-term goals.

Boosting capacity to make optimal strategic investment decisions

In light of the substantial shift in regulatory expectations described in these sections, parties will have to develop capacities to understand investment choices in light of strategic priorities. For the first time, the regulated company is being asked to consider how investment choices are optimal on a whole-system, whole-life basis. To do so, the company must ensure that it can produce robust investment appraisals and understand trade-offs in a way that drives progress towards strategic objectives. Members of the IPPG must also have a firm grasp of the issues involved in expanding decision making to include carbon, natural capital, and social capital. Scottish Water, the regulator, and the IPPG will need to understand the performance of the new approach to investment decision making, expanding existing indicators to measure results in new areas.

WICS envisions a high level of internal scrutiny within Scottish Water feeding into investment, complemented by a level of external scrutiny from the IPPG. After going through internal checks, Scottish Water will publish all of its investment appraisals to a portal for the IPPG to review. The regulator has indicated that they would like to see the company attain a level of internal scrutiny that is so robust, the IPPG stops saying "no." Reaching this point will require the development of capacity within the company, as well as an injection of strategic vision into decision making to allow the company to make trade-offs. The work with experts described in the Challenges associated with long-life assets and time-inconsistency of investment need marked an early stage of the transition period towards a company with the internal capacities to fully meet expectations.

Finding the balance between robust external scrutiny and Scottish Water ownership

WICS has asked Scottish Water to take ownership over its strategy and decisions, and the IPPG should allow the company to preserve ownership if it shows good-faith and well-evidenced reasoning. The role of the government in the IPPG is worth a second look in light of OECD guidance on the governance of state-owned enterprises. The OECD Guidelines on Corporate Governance of State-Owned Enterprises state "the state should act as an informed and active owner" of state-owned enterprises, while allowing such enterprises "full operational autonomy to achieve their defined objectives" and refraining "from intervening in SOE management" (OECD, 2015, p. 20[31]). There is potentially a risk that the IPPG will allow the Scottish Government and other involved parties an inappropriate level of influence in the day-to-day operations of the company. There is a delicate balance to be struck between robust external scrutiny of Scottish Water's investment decision making and micromanagement of the company's operations.

Countering uncertainty for quality regulators

WICS regulates the sector alongside DWQR and SEPA, and a shift away from a list of projects to a more flexible approach could reduce the certainty for quality regulators the previous approach provided. The potential benefits for drinking water and environmental quality that could arise from an economic regulatory framework that looks long-term and bases investment decision making on value instead of cost are significant. However, early resistance to the idea of a flexible investment framework came from the perspective that certain hard requirements must be met for the company to comply with water quality and environmental regulations. In previous price reviews, quality regulators worked with Scottish Water to define investment priorities from water and environmental quality perspectives. Priority projects joined the list, which offered a degree of certainty about the improvements that Scottish Water would make during the regulatory period that followed.

Maintaining buy-in from quality regulators going forward will require a higher burden of proof: not only will the regulatory framework need to deliver expected levels of compliance with standards, but also it will have to demonstrate that it is providing benefits beyond compliance. Consideration for these potential benefits would need to be taken into consideration and evidenced from the very beginning of any investment project and assessed on a continuous basis as projects are implemented. The new approach lacks the surety of the previous approach, and analytical rigour and transparency measures will be important to manage the risk that quality regulators raise a red flag.

Embedding the customer and community voice

The starting point: A commitment to improve opportunities for customer and community input

The price-setting process is high-stakes in the Scottish water sector – affecting a large number of consumers for many years, even beyond the regulatory period – which makes incorporating customer and community views into decision making of critical importance. Stakeholder engagement is a key input to ensure regulations are designed and implemented in the public interest, and the OECD Best Practice Principles on the Governance of Regulators suggests that regulators structure opportunities for engagement in order to favour active participation and exchange of data (OECD, 2014[32]). The mechanisms regulators use to solicit relevant views range widely – including formal public consultation, consultative councils, and customer research.

Formal requirements for the Scottish SRC regulatory process provide limited opportunities for customer engagement. The process invited formal public comment at two junctures during the process: on the draft Ministerial Objectives and Principles of Charging and on WICS's draft determination. WICS considered that such engagement often occurred "after the fact," once major decisions had been made, leaving only marginal opportunities for customer and community involvement. The introduction of a Customer Forum in the previous price review added a new opportunity for constructive challenge during SRC15. In SRC21, WICS would consider new ways to maximise the utility of the Customer Forum as a conduit for customer views in the process.

Research provides another channel for customer views into the SRC process, and it was identified as an area for development in SRC21. Earlier customer research designed to channel insights about customer needs and preferences often fell short of WICS's expectations. A regulatory approach that encouraged long-term thinking introduced a new challenge, requiring an understanding of customers' long-term preferences and evolving attitudes. At the outset of SRC21, WICS sought to explore new ways to better gauge customer views through research, as well as developing the mechanism to translate and incorporate insights into the regulatory process.

The following sections present the mechanisms in SRC21 designed to better represent customer and community voices within the process and during the regulatory period to follow. One section introduces the Customer Forum for SRC21, re-envisioned for SRC21 to have an enhanced role. The second section presents Scottish Water's plan to use a new customer group to take forward its commitment to act "as though there is a customer in the room," pushing beyond simple consultation to bring the customer and community voice into the company. The third section explores how a Research Co-ordination Group for SRC21 was involved in the research feeding into SRC21, including research using innovative methods like behavioural insights.

Moving ahead: New and improved mechanisms for engagement and research

The Customer Forum amplifies the customer voice within SRC21, with an evolving mandate

Inspired by the success of the Customer Forum in the previous price review, SRC21 would also feature a Customer Forum for SRC21 to provide a conduit for customer views and negotiating Scottish Water's business plan. WICS defined a broader remit for the Customer Forum in SRC21, with the additional task of reaching out to communities across Scotland to understand their priorities and working with Scottish Water on other customer research. During SRC21, the Customer Forum joined other key stakeholders in Stakeholder Advisory Group meetings (discussed further in The multi-lateral governance of SRC21 creates new opportunity for exchange).

A tripartite co-operation agreement between CAS, Scottish Water and WICS established the Customer Forum for SRC21. The agreement, published as an Appendix to WICS's methodology document, reaffirmed the role of the Forum to act as a conduit for customers' views rather than being representative of customers or reflecting the users' demographics, similarly to SRC15. The new Customer Forum retained half of the members (including the then-Chair) from the previous price review, guaranteeing some experience and continuity from SRC15.

The co-operation agreement set out the Customer Forum's responsibilities for SRC21:

- working with Scottish Water on research to establish customers' priorities;
- ensuring that the research programme includes a meaningful level of engagement from communities;
- understanding and representing to WICS and Scottish Water the priorities and preferences of customers; and
- seeking to ensure the most appropriate outcome for consumers (both now and into the future) based on those priorities and preferences, in particular by seeking to establish an agreed Business Plan (WICS, 2017[3]).

To accompany the shift from a business plan to a strategic plan, WICS adjusted the mandate of the Forum. The Forum would seek to agree two things with Scottish Water:

- whether Scottish Water adequately takes into account in its Strategic Plan the Customer Forum's evidence on customer views and aspirations, and
- a price profile to deliver the Strategic Plan, within limits defined by WICS (WICS, 2018[16]).

In line with these expectations, the Forum and Scottish Water reached a draft agreement on prices in March 2020.

In response to the unfolding COVID-19 pandemic, the Customer Forum's role shifted once again in spring 2020. As infections rose and the government imposed lockdowns across the UK, the Customer Forum and Scottish Water expressed concern about taking price decisions without better understanding of the impact of the pandemic. WICS adjusted its approach to respond to this uncertainty: it took setting a fixed price profile for the regulatory period off the table, to be replaced with a more flexible approach. Therefore, the Customer Forum's anticipated role in agreeing the maximum amount of charges and negotiating price profiles with Scottish Water was no longer necessary. Instead, in April 2020, WICS asked the Forum to engage with Scottish Water focusing on two questions:

- How should Scottish Water's Transformation Plan reflect customers' expectations?
- How should Scottish Water deliver on its commitment to become more customer-centric and community focused? (WICS, 2020, p. 17[23]).

Not all Customer Forum members were pleased with this new direction, and this and other concurrent events struck a blow to the trust that had developed between the Forum, the company and the regulator. The change in mandate came as the United Kingdom was experiencing its worst impacts from the COVID-19 pandemic to date, and questions arose about the ability of customers to absorb increased prices. In addition, information that Scottish Water had significant cash reserves surfaced in the same month, attracting critique in the media about WICS's perceived "overcharging" (The Scotsman, 2021[33]). After these changes and details came to light, the chair of the Customer Forum resigned in late April 2020. Under its new chair, the Customer Forum took forward the questions posed by WICS, drafting a "Minute of Agreement on the Customer Forum's Expectations of Scottish Water's Transformation Plan". The document expresses the Forum's expectations for the transformation required across the company to deliver its high-level strategic objectives.

While a changing mandate caused discomfort for the Forum and an agreement on prices between the Forum and Scottish Water negotiated was not ultimately used, the group still managed to deliver value in key areas. The Forum released a summary of its achievements during SRC21. It highlighted the engagement of the Forum in SRC21, including through its participation in stakeholder and working groups, its engagement during "deep dive" sessions, and its release of Forum position papers. Among its achievements, the Forum noted its role in crafting the vision and strategic plan, its early championing for climate change as a key strategic issue, and its role in securing Scottish Water's commitment to customer centricity. In addition, the Forum notes that it delivered upon its final mandate, successfully reaching an agreement with Scottish Water on its expectations for the company's transformation plan (Customer Forum, 2020[34]).

Scottish Water establishes a new conduit for customer views

The Customer Forum formally came to an end with the completion of the SRC process in 2020. Going forward, CAS would continue to be the voice of customer on water policy matters, until the newly-created Consumer Scotland takes its place in this area.[1] However, stakeholders judged that neither the Forum nor CAS could effectively support efforts by Scottish Water to involve customers and communities as stated in the Strategic Plan, giving rise to discussions of new forms of engagement and empowerment in order to give customers a voice in the investment process. A new customer group under the ownership of Scottish Water held the promise of ensuring Scottish Water recognised the expectation to go beyond traditional customer engagement.

2020 saw several discussions about the potential shape that a conduit for a customer voice might take post-SRC21. In March 2020, the Stakeholder Advisory Group considered a Scottish Water discussion paper on the future Customer Forum. The discussion paper defines the key principles upon which a future group may be based, including that it be hosted by Scottish Water while retaining its operational independence within the policy framework set by the Scottish Government (Scottish Water, 2020[35]).

In the course of discussions between Scottish Water and the Customer Forum, the company and the customer conduit came to an agreement on certain elements of a new Independent Customer Group (ICG), spelled out in the Minute of Agreement on expectations for the Transformation Plan. They echo the discussion paper, confirming that the group will be operationally independent within Scottish Water. They agree on the remit of the ICG, whose functions will include partnering with Scottish Water to develop and implement an engagement programme. The ICG maintains a challenge function; the agreement states that plans submitted to approval from the government, WICS, or CAS will also be submitted to the customer group for their comments. For continuity, an interim customer group was constituted from the existing membership of the Customer Forum. The interim group functioned until the new ICG was inaugurated in spring 2021 (Scottish Water, 2021[36]).

Stakeholders created the Research Co-ordination Group (RCG) to ensure effective co-ordination of the research feeding into SRC21. The research would fall under the SRC21 research programme, designed to identify customer priorities and preferences. By promoting information sharing and feedback, a more streamlined research programme than under SRC15 was expected.

 The terms of reference for the group envisioned the participation of representatives from Scottish Water, the Customer Forum (which would also chair the group), and CAS's Consumers Futures Unit. In practice, WICS and stakeholders also participated in the group. The three establishing parties each contributed something different to the research feeding into SRC21: the RCG's terms of reference stated that the activities under the research programme would include CFU research for policy purposes, Scottish Water's customer research, additional research commissioned by the Customer Forum, and other relevant research. The group operated with an 'open data' approach, sharing the results (often at an early stage) of research for SRC21.

Initially, most of the research considered by the RCG originated with one actor, with CAS or Scottish Water taking the lead on studies individually. Over time, more collaborative research has been developed. For example, Scottish Water and the Customer Forum collaborated on two activities: legacy research designed to understand how customers want to be regarded by future generations and wider environment research designed to understand customer attitudes towards Scottish Water's environmental responsibilities. In addition, CAS, Scottish Water and the Customer Forum conducted research into successful community engagement practices.

The RCG reported to the Stakeholder Advisory Group regularly, and the RCG's decisions on research activities have reflected key themes unfolding in the SRC process. The focus of the research programme has evolved, with earlier research investigating matters of short-term, personal impact and later research displaying a longer-term focus. Scottish Water's customer research programme, Engage 21, follows this trend. Early Engage 21 research assessed customer priorities through research involving retail customers, licensed providers and community councils. During the second phase of Engage 21, Scottish Water's research focused on specific issues related to operations, such as water pressure, wastewater, and lead in water. At later stages, the research has tackled questions of strategy, investigating community engagement, legacy, and the wider environment. This evolution followed developments in SRC21, with the shift to a strategic plan creating greater need and opportunity for research of a more strategic nature.

As the SRC progressed, the RCG took steps to ensure that the group prioritised high-impact research with greater potential to materially affect SRC21. The RCG held an independently facilitated workshop in December 2018 to agree on research priorities for the remainder of the SRC process. Stakeholders distilled 39 research priorities into three priority themes:

- pricing and willingness to pay,

- legacy, and

- relative importance of environmental impacts and service quality considerations.

Faced with a small window of opportunity for research to influence SRC21 outcomes, the RCG took action to ensure that the research programme provided coverage of important issues.

The Group also agreed to trial innovative research methods such as behavioural insights and deliberative research. The behaviourally informed research (discussed further in Box 3.2) presented the opportunity to go beyond traditional research methods to explore underlying motivations and biases using empirical methods. The use of behaviourally-informed research to better understand customer preferences was one of the innovations foreseen by WICS to provide better research inputs into SRC21 (Water Industry Commission for Scotland, 2017[37]). Deliberative research, which allowed participants to engage with the facilitator and the responses of other participants, generated more subtle insights on how customer views on Scottish Water's strategy change when presented with additional information about the sector and the challenges it faces.

Box 3.6. Behavioural research provides insights on customers' perceptions of long-term prices

Price setting conducted by economic regulators has significant and lasting impacts, making the quality of input on customer priorities critical. Behavioural insights (BI) research presents an opportunity to explore underlying motivations and biases of participants, allowing the regulator to understand and address biases when designing interventions and anticipate potential pitfalls. The research provides a perspective that is a valuable companion to other research inputs to regulatory processes, like polling research.

The Economic and Social Research Institute (ESRI) produced behavioural insights studies to deepen understanding of behavioural factors that influence customer attitudes. Both studies, described below, involved an online survey and face-to-face laboratory study with participants from across Scotland.

Study 1: Measuring attitudes towards water charges and different price trajectories for future charges.

The study started by testing participants' priors about acceptable price changes, showing that the largest group of participants preferred no price change, followed by a price increase, and then a price decrease. The study then tested how the size and the presentation of price trajectories affects their acceptability, finding that the greatest number of participants preferred a smooth upward price trajectory, followed by a front-loaded, then back-loaded. The final stage tested whether providing additional information affected participants' acceptance of price trajectories, with results suggesting that providing information about annual costs resulted in a preference for front-loaded trajectories, followed by constant, and finally by back-loaded. When participants were given figures on total (cumulative) costs, there was no longer a significant preference for front-loaded and constant trajectories.

Study 2: Trade-offs between costs and benefits of additional investment in the Scottish water industry

The first stage asked participants to rank seven benefits in order of importance, including four target benefits (reducing interruptions to supply, reducing external sewer flooding, connecting rural supplies to the water system, and increasing the share of renewable energy generated by the water industry). Results did not show that any one benefit was more important at this stage. Next, participants were asked to allocate an unknown amount of money between the four target improvements. Here, participants allocated the most money to external sewer flooding, followed by renewable energy, interruptions to supply and rural supplies.

In the third stage, participants were asked to state the maximum amount of money they would be willing to add to their current water bill if they knew the revenue would be used towards the four target improvements. On average, participants were willing to add £11.03 to their water bills (an increase of around 2.5% in the bills). However, 40% of participants indicated that they were unwilling to add any additional amount to their charges.

In the fourth stage, the experimenters revealed the costs of the target improvements. The participants could manipulate the amount they would be willing to add to their bill and the percent allocation to each benefit. The programme told participants how much of the improvements would result if everyone invested the same amount. In this stage, participants' percent allocations remained about the same, but 14% of participants increased their water charge. The final stage added time horizons, indicating whether benefits would be delivered immediately, in five years, in ten years or in 25 years. This stage saw a significant increase in allocation towards immediate benefits.

> Among the results of this study, one result stands out: the study suggested that participants were willing to pay more for the benefits. Participants were especially willing to pay more for short-term benefits when they knew the time horizons of each benefit (Belton, Lavin and Lunn, 2020[38]).
>
> Source: Belton, C., C. Lavin, and P. Lunn (2020), Eliciting trade-offs between water charges and service benefits in Scotland. ESRI Working Paper No. 655. https://www.esri.ie/system/files/publications/WP655_1.pdf.

The RCG also experimented a tool for quick tactical sampling to complement the research programme. The RCG first experimented with the use of a chatbot, partnering with Apptivism to solicit the public's views on water issues through three chats with a Facebook Messenger chatbot. Faced with mixed success in the chats and Apptivism's inability to accept further commissions, the RCG decided not to continue with a chatbot. The RCG agreed that other data collection methods could continue to serve as ways to gauge customer preferences, such as traditional omnibus surveys.

Looking forward: The challenges of embedding the customer and community voice

Extending beyond business-as-usual consultation, including through the use of behaviourally-informed approaches, represents a significant change to the way customer engagement has been conducted in the Scottish water sector. Attempts to better represent customer and community views in the SRC process and decision making during the regulatory period have met some challenges. Notably, WICS and stakeholders faced the persisting view of engagement as a continuation of business-as-usual consultation and the lack of shared understanding of a "community" view.

Expanding beyond normal consultation

While WICS had a view of ongoing, integral engagement from the beginning of SRC21, the regulator identified moving beyond viewing engagement as business-as-usual consultation as a challenge. After several years of discussion, the outputs of SRC21 show a commitment to ramping up engagement during the regulatory period. The commitment of Scottish Water to make every decision as though "the customer were in the room" represented a formal commitment to push beyond existing consultation methodologies. Furthermore, the ICG serves to institutionalise engagement, with the promise of engagement becoming more continuous and integral.

The challenge going forward will be to further develop the capacities to solicit and react to the full range of stimuli from customers and communities, including public empowerment. While stakeholders lack a shared definition of "empowerment," public participation literature such as the International Association for Public Participation's Spectrum of Public Participation presents public empowerment as the most participative mode of engagement, where the public adopts a decision making role. WICS hopes to see, and Scottish Water has committed to show, a more proactive exchange with customers and communities that extends beyond engagement to empowerment. Stakeholders have raised the bar, expecting that the company will have to think "outside the box" to broaden the approach. This represents considerably heightened ambition compared to engagement strategies during previous regulatory periods, and the challenge of embedding the customer and community voice has featured in conversations about Scottish Water's transformation.

The commitment to deepening the connection between decision making and customer and community voices is only the first step towards customer centricity, and Scottish Water has a range of tools to advance its goal. The ICG will be one tool to channel customer and community voices into decision making. Certain tools show greater promise to collect new information on customer preferences: behavioural and deliberative research provided interesting insights and could be used more systematically, while other methods like the use of chatbots proved less useful in surveying preferences. Scottish Water is also considering which internal changes will enable a receptive and empathetic approach to customer- and community-facing actions, and ultimately community and customer empowerment.

Maximising the utility of the ICG, while recognising its limitations

The ICG can be seen as an early step towards embedding EBP in Scottish Water's operations, and certain elements can help ensure that it is best placed to provide useful information. The ICG's effectiveness hinges on its ability to channel customer and community voices, as discussed above, but also its capacity to maintain adequate challenge. The group is not stand-alone like the Customer Forum, but instead is housed within Scottish Water. It is still envisioned as an independent body; the ICG's ToR states that the group will be "operationally independent... free from any perceived capture" and also "adequately resourced". While the ToR lays the foundations for independent decision making, the ICG may contend with a reputational risk if stakeholders perceive it to be constrained, controlled or captured going forward. Like the Customer Forum, the ICG does not claim to be representative of the Scottish population. This approach presents another risk: if participants do not appropriately acknowledge and manage the natural biases of the group, it risks replicating its biases in the information it produces.

Ensuring research has high-impact results

Timing is key to ensure that research comes at the best moment to feed into the process. While earlier research by members of the RCG served a scoping function, participants initially lacked a framework to understand where to invest time and resources to ensure that research was high-impact. While desk research conducted in 2017 identified existing research with relevant results for SRC21, a structured conversation about research priorities did not take place until late 2018. The timing of later studies, such as the deliberative research conducted in late 2018, limited the impact on SRC21.

The ICG has taken early steps towards a research approach grounded in a framework that helps the group target high-impact and timely research questions. In August 2021, the ICG re-established the Research Co-ordination Group. Its purpose, according to the group, is "to facilitate coordination and collaboration among water sector stakeholders on research designed to elicit a comprehensive understanding of customers and communities' needs and aspirations." The group has expressed its intention to develop a research framework to guide its actions.

The research programme also could have benefitted from an early and deliberate consideration of its scope to ensure that research reflected areas of highest value. The agreement establishing the Customer Forum sketched out an early view of the scope of the research programme, encompassing "high quality, behavioural, quantitative and qualitative research within the context of the SRC to establish customers' priorities for service level improvement and expectations in terms of the level of charges" (WICS, 2017, p. 80[15]). Within this broad mandate, the research programme involved a wide range of research questions and research methodologies. Being driven by a small group of insiders, a risk is that the research programme replicates the personal or organisational views of participants, potentially failing to produce research in areas of highest value and of greatest importance to customers. A more deliberate approach incorporating external challenge could reduce the opportunity for design bias.

Establishing shared understanding of what a community view of engagement means

While the regulator and stakeholders were adamant that the company engage both customers and communities, initially the group had no shared understanding of how a community view could translate into decision making. From the beginning of SRC21, outward-facing messaging about SRC21 expressed that SRC21 would capture the needs of and deliver benefits for "customers and communities" (see, e.g. WICS (2017[3])). To clarify expectations, Scottish Water asked stakeholders to explain what was meant by engaging customers and communities in the process.

The Customer Forum, following a discussion with CAS/CFU, released a short response to Scottish Water in 2018. In the paper, they present their view on how the company can better engage, including with communities of place and communities of interest. These terms represent two different ways of conceptualising community: while communities of place are bound by geography, communities of interest bring together people around shared interests (Robinson and Green, 2011[39]). The Customer Forum suggests a range of methods to engage communities of place, including conducting targeted research that yields local insights and co-creating plans for local interventions. To engage communities of interest, the Forum suggests the creation of panels catering to specific interests, including groups representative of vulnerable populations, young people, the elderly, and environment and recreation interests.

Note

[1] The Consumer Scotland Act 2020 creates a new consumer advocacy and support body, Consumer Scotland (Scottish Parliament, 2020[40]). The functions that were previously held by CAS in the water sector will be conducted by Consumer Scotland.

References

Ahearn, T. (2020), *Response: Strategic Review of Charges 2021-27 – Draft Determination*, Letter to Alan Sutherland, Chief Executive of WICS, https://www.watercommission.co.uk/UserFiles/Documents/SEPA_Redacted.pdf (accessed on 17 December 2020). [30]

Belton, C., C. Lavin and P. Lunn (2020), *Eliciting trade-offs between water charges and service benefits in Scotland.*, https://www.esri.ie/system/files/publications/WP655_1.pdf. [38]

CAS (2020), *Citizens Advice Scotland Response to 'Strategic Review of Charges 2021-27: Draft Determination'*, https://www.cas.org.uk/system/files/publications/202011_final_cas_response_to_draft_deter mination_2021-27.pdf (accessed on 16 December 2020). [29]

Citizens Advice Scotland (2021), *Full Disclosure: The use of Third Party Intermediaries within Scotland's water market*, https://www.cas.org.uk/system/files/publications/insight_report_tpis_april_2021.pdf. [9]

Customer Forum (2020), *The Customer Forum in SR21: A Brief Summary*, https://d1ssu070pg2v9i.cloudfront.net/pex/customerforum/2020/10/05165025/The-Forum-in-SRC21-a-brief-summary-final.pdf. [34]

Hendry, S. (2016), "The customer forum - Putting customers at the centre of regulating water services", *Water Policy*, Vol. 18/4, pp. 948-963, https://doi.org/10.2166/wp.2016.199. [2]

Hodges, C. and R. Steinholtz (2017), *Ethical Business Practice and Regulation: A Behavioural and Values-Based Approach to Compliance and Enforcement*, Hart Publishing, Oxford, https://www.bloomsburyprofessional.com/uk/ethical-business-practice-and-regulation-9781509916368/ (accessed on 23 March 2021). [5]

Mayer, C. (2018), *Editorial: Averting corporate crises*, pp. 3-5,
https://www.thebritishacademy.ac.uk/documents/348/BAR34-02-Mayer-Editorial.pdf
(accessed on 24 March 2021). [7]

Millican, D. (2020), *Response: Strategic Review of Charges 2021-27 – Draft Determination*,
Letter to Alan Sutherland, Chief Executive of WICS,
https://wics.scot/system/files/publications/2021-27%20Responses.pdf (accessed on
17 December 2020). [28]

OECD (2015), *OECD Guidelines on Corporate Governance of State-Owned Enterprises, 2015
Edition*, OECD Publishing, Paris, https://doi.org/10.1787/9789264244160-en. [31]

OECD (2014), *The Governance of Regulators*, OECD Best Practice Principles for Regulatory
Policy, OECD Publishing, Paris, https://doi.org/10.1787/9789264209015-en. [32]

Robinson, J. and G. Green (2011), "Developing Communities", in Robinson, J. and G. Green
(eds.), *Introduction to Community Development*. [39]

Scottish Government (2020), *Water services - charging principles: 2021 to 2027*,
https://www.gov.scot/publications/principles-of-charging-2021-2027/ (accessed on
4 May 2021). [20]

Scottish Government (2019), *Protecting Scotland's Future: the Government's Programme for
Scotland 2019-2020*, https://www.gov.scot/publications/protecting-scotlands-future-
governments-programme-scotland-2019-20/pages/5/. [24]

Scottish Parliament (2020), *Consumer Scotland Act*, https://www.legislation.gov.uk/asp/2020/11. [40]

Scottish Water (2021), *Minute of Agreement between Scottish Water and the Customer Forum
on Expectations for the Transformation Plan*, https://www.scottishwater.co.uk/About-
Us/News-and-Views/2021/04/280421-ICG (accessed on 6 July 2022). [36]

Scottish Water (2020), *Asset Management Transformation Routemap, V1.1*. [18]

Scottish Water (2020), *Future Customer Forum Discussion Paper*, Internal paper,
https://scottishwater365.sharepoint.com/:w:/r/sites/externalprojects/src21/_layouts/15/doc.asp
x?sourcedoc=%7b8702a449-5e93-4a7a-b322-
43c0e9fc603e%7d&file=future%20customer%20forum_for%20sag%20v7.docx&action=defau
lt&mobileredirect=true&defaultitemopen=1 (accessed on 19 September 2020). [35]

Scottish Water (2018), *Shaping the future of your water and wastewater services.*,
https://www.scottishwater.co.uk/-/media/ScottishWater/Document-Hub/Key-
Publications/Reports/211218shapingthefutureoutcomesreport.pdf (accessed on 6 July 2022). [21]

Scottish Water (n.d.), *Net Zero Emissions Routemap*,
https://scottishwaternetzero.co.uk/reducing-emissions/ (accessed on 11 July 2021). [25]

Scottish Water and Customer Forum (2020), *Minute of Agreement on the Strategic Plan*,
https://www.scottishwater.co.uk/-/media/ScottishWater/Document-Hub/Key-
Publications/Strategic-Plan/300120StrategicPlanMinuteofAgreement.pdf (accessed on
6 July 2022). [22]

SEPA (2016), *One Planet Prosperity - Our Regulatory Strategy*, https://www.sepa.org.uk/media/219427/one-planet-prosperity-our-regulatory-strategy.pdf (accessed on 29 September 2020). [14]

Sutherland, A. (2021), *The good, the bad and the ugly: How might we future proof economic regulation?*. [1]

The Scotsman (2021), *Scottish Water under fire over £391m cash reserves as prices rise. Retrieved June 29, 2021*, https://www.scotsman.com/news/politics/scottish-water-under-fire-over-ps391m-cash-reserves-prices-rise-3110184 (accessed on 29 June 2021). [33]

The Water Report (2019), *Scotland's water sector co-creates vision with social purpose*, https://www.thewaterreport.co.uk/single-post/2019/10/20/scotland-s-water-sector-co-creates-vision-with-social-purpose (accessed on 6 July 2022). [8]

Water Industry Commission for Scotland (2017), *Innovation and Collaboration: future proofing the water industry for customers*. [37]

WICS (2021), *Corporate Plan 2021-27*, https://www.watercommission.co.uk/UserFiles/Documents/WICS_CorporatePlan2021-27_4Dec.pdf. [13]

WICS (2021), *Measures in support of the retail market in light of the current pandemic*, https://www.watercommission.co.uk/UserFiles/Documents/Consultation%20on%20Measures%20in%20Support%20of%20the%20Retail%20Market%20in%20Light%20of%20the%20Current%20Pandemic.pdf. [11]

WICS (2021), *Measures in support of the retail market in light of the current pandemic - call for consultations*, https://www.watercommission.co.uk/UserFiles/Documents/Consultation%20on%20Measures%20in%20Support%20of%20the%20Retail%20Market%20in%20Light%20of%20the%20Current%20Pandemic.pdf. [12]

WICS (2020), *Consultation Responses*, https://www.watercommission.co.uk/view_Consultation_Responses.aspx (accessed on 17 December 2020). [27]

WICS (2020), *Draft Determination: Strategic Review of Charges 2021-27*, https://www.watercommission.co.uk/UserFiles/Documents/Strategic Review of Charges 2021-27 Draft Determination_1.pdf. [23]

WICS (2020), *Final Determination: Strategic Review of Charges 2021-27*, https://www.watercommission.co.uk/UserFiles/Documents/WICS%20Final%20Determination%20Report%20-%20Final%20Screen%20ready%20for%20website_1.pdf (accessed on 16 December 2020). [6]

WICS (2020), *Impact of COVID-19 on the Strategic Review of Charges 2021-27*. [19]

WICS (2020), *Measures in support of the retail market in light of the current pandemic*, https://www.watercommission.co.uk/UserFiles/documents/Letter%20on%20Measure%20in%20Response%20to%20Covid-19_1.pdf. [10]

WICS (2020), *Prospects for Prices Strategic Review of Charges 2021-27 Final Decision Paper*, https://wics.scot/system/files/publications/Prospects%20for%20prices.pdf (accessed on 6 July 2022). [4]

WICS (2018), *Capital Maintenance*, http://www.watercommission.co.uk (accessed on 22 September 2020). [17]

WICS (2018), *Investment planning and prioritisation*, http://www.watercommission.co.uk (accessed on 22 September 2020). [26]

WICS (2018), *Strategic Review of Charges 2021-27: Methodology refinements and clarifications*, http://www.watercommission.co.uk/ (accessed on 18 February 2021). [16]

WICS (2017), *Innovation and Collaboration: future proofing the water industry for customers*. [3]

WICS (2017), *Innovation and Collaboration: future proofing the water industry for customers*, https://www.watercommission.co.uk/UserFiles/Documents/SRC21_Innovation%20and%20Collaboration_Methodology_WICS_amended.pdf (accessed on 25 March 2021). [15]

Annex A. Regulator decision papers

Through regular decision papers, WICS communicates its evolving understanding and expectations for the regulatory process. Between June 2017 and February 2020, WICS published a series of Decision Papers outlining its views on key parameters for the Strategic Review of Charges. The Decision Papers "sought to build a common understanding of the key regulatory inputs and the likely challenges the industry will face in 2020-21 period and long into the future" (WICS, 2020[1]). These papers, published on the regulator's website, served to provide technical information to the stakeholders involved in the SRC.

The first batch of thirteen Initial Decision Papers was published between August and October 2017. They touched on a wide-ranging set of issues and put forward various options to address them, both in the current SRC and beyond. Initial Decision Paper 2 made clear that Scottish Water would likely have to invest more in future regulatory periods (WICS, 2020[1]). The Initial Decision Paper 7 on sustainable asset maintenance highlighted one of the key issues, discussing the challenge that Scottish Water invests sufficiently in maintaining its asset base both in SRC21 and into the future.

Throughout 2018, the Commission published eight Revised Decision Papers which reaffirmed and codified some of the key principles set out in the Methodology, but also captured the evolution joint stakeholder understanding of the issues as multilateral meetings continued. Based on the feedback received on its Revised Papers and the new Commissioning Letter from June 2019, WICS has adopted a more iterative and consultative approach to the drafting of its Final Decision Papers.

In summary, each of the 2018 revised decision papers addressed the following:

- DP1 provided the Commission's comments to Scottish Water's Strategic Projections
- DP2 confirmed the key macroeconomic assumptions outlined in 2017, while recognising that economic uncertainty may require changes in the Final DP.
- DP3 outlined the Commission's expectations around the new investment planning and prioritisation framework required to appraise new investment
- DP4 established a set of expectations in relation to meeting the long-term investment challenge, providing Scottish Water with a list of key questions to think about in relation to developing trust in its new approach to investment
- DP5 focused on a coherent financial approach to capital maintenance, noting that it was very positive to see Scottish Water engage with stakeholders regularly on this issue. It asked Scottish Water to consider the possibility of "ring-fencing" a portion of its allowed revenue, setting this aside for investment pending assurance that the investment would be delivered efficiently and effectively and consistent with addressing the long-term asset challenge.
- DP6 outlined the Commission's expectations on performance reporting, highlighting that greater visibility and transparency of performance can enable Scottish Water to build the trust of customers, communities and other stakeholders
- DP7 confirmed that the Commission expected Scottish Water to use the financial tramlines approach for its recurring expenditure
- DP8 provided a first opportunity for the Commission to write that charges would likely have to increase above the rate of CPI inflation during the following two regulatory control periods

The suite of 2018 decision papers was followed by one 2019 decision paper on asset replacement, and a 2020 final decision paper on prices.

WICS's decision paper on asset replacement

WICS published its Decision Paper on asset replacement challenge in July 2019. This Decision Paper reaffirmed the importance of Scottish Water being sufficiently funded in order to undertake the investment that it needs to make improvements in water quality, environmental compliance and meeting the climate change challenge.

The paper developed earlier positions by WICS on the need to replace assets in light of Scottish Water's net zero targets. In order to do so, it recognised that priority investment should go forward expeditiously and that replacement of medium life assets should take between 8-16 years. It also aligned 2045 as the target year for a smooth transition that takes into account both the replacement of long-life assets and the net zero targets.

This paper benefited from emerging analysis of asset conditions and lives by Scottish Water – WICS praised the company for their continued efforts in these areas and encouraged them to pursue the asset management improvement plan.

Final decision paper: "Prospects for Prices"

WICS' Final Decision Paper, "Prospects for Prices," summarises WICS' views on the appropriate range for charge caps for the upcoming regulatory period (WICS, 2020[1]). Based on the latest DP8, the Commission prepared a draft version of the final Decision Paper on prices and presented this to stakeholders in February 2019 as a slide pack for discussion. The Commission's modelling of asset lives, enhancement needs, growth forecasts and the scope for efficiencies led to an estimated allowance for investment (in growth, replacement and enhancements) of between £870 and £1020 million a year (in 2017-18 prices).

The final version of the paper concluded that average annual charges must increase by between 1% and 2% above CPI inflation to deliver this scale of investment, with an increase in the upper half of that range being most consistent with the magnitude of the long-term challenges facing Scottish Water. It asks the Customer Forum to negotiate with Scottish Water on three issues: investment, an efficiency challenge, and an allowance for potential additional cash outlays for the successful inclusion of emissions in appraisals. It defines the ranges for discussion of each:

1. Targeted annual investment of between £1.0 and £1.1 Billion (in 2017 prices) by 2040.
2. An annual efficiency challenge of between 0.75% and 1.5% for Scottish Water's expenditure on operations (including repairs and routine maintenance), financing and PPP management.
3. An allowance for the potential additional cash outlays (from £0 million to £150 million annually) that could result from including emissions in appraisals (WICS, 2020[1]).

The Commission also regarded that a transition over at least three regulatory control periods would lead to a point where Scottish Water has an appropriate level of annual investment funding to meet those needs. Those funding needs and the estimated transition period translate into a price increase of between 2.7% and 2.9% in nominal terms (0.7% and 0.9% in real terms) for a period of up to 23 years.

In a subsequent meeting (Stakeholder Advisory Group, March 2019) the Commission presented different scenarios of the prospects for future prices in response to comments received from stakeholders. The 'base case' confirms the price ranges and the length of the transition first presented in the slide pack. However, five other scenarios show how prices may be lower or higher depending on the enhancement spending allowed. In all cases, prices would rise above inflation. Scottish Water would be subject to an efficiency challenge of between 1-1.5%.

The paper also stresses the transformation necessary for Scottish Water to meet the dual challenges of net zero emissions and asset replacement. WICS stresses Scottish Water's role in its own transformation and its ownership over its own strategy. It emphasises the importance of evidencing change in the absence of the traditional hard budget constraint to provide stakeholders confidence that the company is making progress towards long-term goals. It notes that Scottish Water should establish a transformation plan to evidence the change within its organisation.

References

Consumer Futures Unit (2018), "Untapped Potential: Consumer Views on Water Policy", https://www.cas.org.uk/publications/untapped-potential-consumer-views-water-policy. [2]

WICS (2020), *Prospects for Prices Strategic Review of Charges 2021-27 Final Decision Paper*, https://wics.scot/system/files/publications/Prospects%20for%20prices.pdf (accessed on 6 July 2022). [1]